STRENGTH

MARINA SHELTON

PAGE PUBLISHING
Conneaut Lake, PA

First originally published by Page Publishing 2024

ISBN 979-8-89157-875-3 (pbk)
ISBN 979-8-89157-876-0 (digital)

Printed in the United States of America

CONTENTS

ACKNOWLEDGEMENTS

I want to thank and acknowledge the people who really inspired me through my recovery and my life. I want to thank my doctors at Boston Medical Center, my doctors and therapists at Spaulding Rehabilitation where I was in Pediatrics and made my recovery, Ross Lilley for getting me involved in all kinds of adapted sports again, Peter and William Halby for getting me involved in adaptive sports and theater, and Mary Demaso for her invaluable editing and support, my agent Phil Drelick, my friends for accepting me, and being so much fun, the people who believed in me, the people who didn't believe in me (motivated me to prove them wrong), and my family for always supporting me and being by my side.

1

WHERE IT ALL BEGAN

My early life was far from average. I was born on March 11, 1993, into a family of five, the youngest of three siblings. My older brother, Neill, and older sister, Lara, kept me on track. They taught me everything from how to escape from my crib by myself when I was still a baby to discovering new opportunities and skills in life.

As the youngest child in my family, I always looked up to Lara and Neill. I wanted to be like them and automatically followed them around to see what they were up to. Sometimes I did so a little too much. I liked to play outside with them and sometimes tried to get involved with them and their friends. I saw how they lived and learned by watching their lifestyles. Neill was then at the middle school, so I didn't see him during the day, but once I started at Loker Elementary School, I saw Lara a little during the school day. She was in fifth grade when I was in kindergarten. Fifth graders were upstairs, and kindergarteners were on the first floor by the school entrance. The high and low grades also had separate playgrounds, yet I still looked for her whenever I could. Some afternoons, Lara would even come down to my kindergarten class and read to us.

In preschool, my life began to extend beyond my family. On the first day, I met a little girl named Jasmine. As that first school day finished and both of our mothers came to take us home, Jasmine was holding one of the *My Little Pony* toys. I already I had a passion for horses and was obsessed with the *My Little Pony* cartoons and toys. To this day, I have an entire volume on DVD. As I smiled, she handed it to me, and we played while our mothers talked. We were having an amazing time. When the time came for them to leave, I was a little reluctant to give back the toy.

"Now, Marina, she came over, and you played with it together. Now they're leaving, so you need to give it back," my mom told me gently but seriously.

That was really my first true friendship in a school setting. I already liked being with people, so, of course, I was all over the place, but because of this interaction, I built a strong friendship with Jasmine. She and I were constantly having playdates and went to each other's birthday parties. I learned to share not only toys but companionship as well. Our friendship represents an early demonstration of both my love of horses and my enthusiasm in getting along with people, both of which contributed in surprising ways to making me who I am today.

As my first years continued, Lara and Neill started studying ballet and, importantly, figure skating. I was still so young that my mom brought me to their skating lessons so that she could see them while still looking after me. In this way, I earned the nickname of a "Rink Rat." As I grew a little older, however, I recognized the beauty and exciting speed of figure skating, the grace of the people I saw glide, spin, and jump, so I started my first basic skills skating lessons when I was three. This was my introduction to a passion and hobby I would enjoy and appreciate throughout my life.

Since our mom was the director and principal teacher of a ballet studio in our hometown of Wayland, Massachusetts, I soon joined Neill and Lara in dancing as well as skating. I began pre-ballet lessons when I was four, learning the beginning ballet basics like pliés and the five ballet positions. All of us appeared in numerous end-of-year demonstrations. The videos showed that I always completed a routine by waving to my grandparents. It was never surprising for my parents to find me dancing around the house.

We all knew that ballet was important to assist in skating. The movements to music in both are crucial. There is much technicality in figure skating element-wise, but the artistry and grace, which ballet provides, is equally as important. I would watch Lara and Neill skating and dancing, falling in love with the combination of music and movement. There was more though. Through ballet, I became familiar with classics, like *Swan Lake* and especially *The Nutcracker*. I learned the music and the general plot lines of traditional ballet stories, such as that of Clara at her family Christmas Eve party where she was gifted with a Nutcracker. Her godfather, Drosselmeyer, worked magic that led to the Nutcracker's coming to life, battling the Rat King and taking Clara on a journey to the Land of Sweets. This was all an important aspect of my life because it introduced me to my love of dance.

When I understood that my whole family danced in Dance Prism's touring ballet company, of course, as the youngest family member would, I'd always ask, "Mommy, Mommy! Can I do that too?" Of course, I wanted to be Clara.

Mom laughed and replied, "Well, Marina, you need to wait until you are a little older, and then you can start."

Similarly, I remember a day when, while watching one of Lara and Neill's practice sessions, I again expressed my enthusiasm for skating. After the lesson, their coach, Felita, walked up to me and asked, "Marina, how old are you?"

"Free!" I answered, still unable to pronounce a "th."

"Well, when you're four, I'll start teaching you how to start skating."

My excitement took me over for the rest of the day. I couldn't wait until I was older to start private lessons. Looking back, the fact that she promised to take me on at such a young age was remarkable.

Meanwhile, the next few years came by leaps and bounds. I had started pre-ballet at my mom's ballet studio, and basic skills skating lessons, which I took at Babson Skating Center in Wellesley. Since I was still so little, I always went to Neill and Lara's skating practices too. Almost every day in my life was a little like this: preschool, Neill and Lara's lessons, ballet, basic skills lessons. Even as I loved all that, I had my moments of doubt. Some days, I did not want to give up skating and dancing, but other times I did. I don't remember why exactly, but I was so young that whenever I didn't feel up to it, I told my mom I didn't want to do that. She was easy about wanting each of us to have our childhood. She said my hesitation was okay and that I didn't have to do it, but that once I was enrolled in something, I needed to see the year through. Well, that made me happy, but the mood never lasted long. It continued for a few weeks, but I still watched as Neill and Lara skated and danced in their lessons. Not surprisingly, that was enough encouragement for me. Not long after, I came around and continued lessons.

I believe that for most people, succeeding through one goal tends to introduce another; at least that is the perspective I have always wanted to take. Growing up watching my older siblings sparked a desire in me to be the best I could be. Whenever I watched them dance, skate, or even do whatever they did in their free time, I always thought to myself, *One day, I'm going to be just as good as they are.* Of course, being like this led me to work twice as hard at everything. I raced the boys in my elementary school, challenged them to a basketball game, and always ran around the rink after my skating lesson to build stamina and endurance.

When I finally started going to the rink on a continuous basis, I got to know the other skaters and began to learn the value of friendships. My family and I became friendly with the family of Drew Meekins, who skated at the same time as Neill and Lara. I met Drew's little brother, Cameron, at the rink, too, when he and his mom, Nancy, came and watched Drew's lessons. The friendship between our two families developed because Cameron and I became friends. As time went on, our friendship grew along with us. When I finished my skating session, after I changed out of my skates and skating dress, we always ran around the rink and had a great time together as good friends would. I recall fondly one specific evening when Cameron, Nancy, and I all went to see the movie *Dude, Where's My Car?* We laughed so hard through the entire movie. That led to a series of inside jokes, mostly based on quotations from the movie whenever Cameron and I saw each other.

"Dude, where's my car?"

"Where's your car, dude?"

"Dude, where's my car?"

For me, it was a great experience that displayed true friendship, on and off the ice. Whenever something was happening with school or I hadn't had my best session, I could always count on Cameron to help me find my smile again. The fact that we were the same age probably contributed to our connection.

I also met Travis, the younger brother of another skater that my sister and I were friendly with. Similarly, he and I ran around the rink together when I wasn't skating a session. Laughter and pure joy always surfaced when we were together. We always looked forward to seeing each other at the rink. Cameron also hung out with us, so we had a complete gang of three literally running around the rink having a great time together. We all had different interests, but we had enough in common that we always enjoyed each other's company. Therefore, the rink to me became like a second with a different kind of family.

Although I loved the look of ice skating and ballet dancing, what I really wanted to do at that time was horseback riding. I was still obsessed with the *My Little Pony* series, entranced by horses in movies and in love with an iridescent white horse whose paddock we passed on the way to Dance Prism rehearsals. Occasionally, when we were going home, my parents would stop the car at one side of the fence. I would excitedly jump out of the car and run up to the fence. Most of the time, one or more of the horses walked over, lifted his head over the fence, and brought it down so that it was reachable for me. I loved it whenever this happened, and I gently ran my hand down his muzzle, stroking down the side of the neck. This only strengthened my love for horses! In those moments, I became determined that one day I would begin horseback riding. The friendships, the family connections, and the early passion for beauty and movement in various forms combined to shape me. Skating, ballet, horses, and the fluidity of that moment all represent who I am. The person I am now is clearly the result of where it all began.

2

EXPERIENCES

Throughout my young life, diverse experiences with school, skating, ballet, travel, and friendships, I almost always had a distraction. In between, I kept myself busy. Being still was never an attractive option.

From earliest childhood, I had fun playing with my hair whenever I was bored. If something was out of reach, my hair was always a good alternative. When I was three, it was long enough that I could twist it around my fingers a couple of times. Whenever I watched TV or someone was visiting, out of habit, I would automatically reach for my hair and twirl the end into my fingers. I was so happy, and the length looked so pretty. I wasn't prepared for what would happen when I got older.

One day, still when I was two, Mom took me to "an appointment." I loved getting out of the house, so I happily went along. When we pulled up to the hair salon, I assumed the cut was for her. But she walked me up to one of the chairs. I looked around, and everything seemed pleasant there. I thought it was cool that I was with adults again and was getting a chance to do "a grown-up" thing. Mom helped me up onto one of the special chairs, and the hairdresser started washing my hair. Of course, I thought all was fine, but when she took out the scissors and cut a small amount of my hair (I was getting a trim), I screamed bloody murder and started sobbing, traumatized at having my precious haircut. Mom was horrified. That performance marked my last haircut for a few years; Mom did not want to go through all that again. I was thrilled with that decision, not understanding that eventually I would need to get it trimmed periodically. In the meantime, my hair grew past my waist. I always imagined styling my hair in a fancy updo when I was older, like the one Rose has in *The Titanic*. I loved having my long hair.

Kindergarten brought new experiences, positive and negative, to my life. Though I had begun to learn to read in preschool, I hadn't known how to read consistently, and I always thought that reading looked boring as opposed to watching TV or playing. When I got the hang of it, however, I actually enjoyed the processes of formulating the words and understanding the stories. More importantly, I discovered that when I read, my vivid imagination would form a series of images in my mind that would finally combine to create an imaginary movie.

My natural creativity also surfaced in my enjoyment of arts and crafts. Thus, one sadly remembered day, I was standing absorbed at the art table drawing some pictures and talking to new friends. The art table consisted of markers, pens, pencils, colored pencils, scissors, glue, and glitter. It should be noted that my beloved long and seldom-trimmed hair was flowing down loosely as I often wore it. I was thoroughly occupied when I heard my friend, Alex, say, "Marina, I cut your hair."

I looked at him for a few seconds, not sure I understood. "No, you didn't."

"Yes, I did," he replied, smirking as he held up a pair of scissors and about half an inch of my hair.

I may have freaked out about my first haircut, but this time, I was really enraged. I couldn't believe that one of my friends had the nerve to do that and then tell me. I had first thought he had been kidding, but after seeing the proof of his boast, I was so livid that I was crying. He, of course, got into deep trouble when our teacher found out, and a few days afterward, I received a package at home with a long apology letter from him and a beautiful hair barrette. Some days later, after my flames of fury burned out, our friendship resumed, surmounting the passing threat to its endurance. My first real conflict ended in peaceful resolution.

Despite such disturbances, the years continued with a number of surprising turns. As young students, we all participated in activities that would grow to become more significant in our school future, such as delivering valentines to friends, dressing up for school on Halloween, and altogether beginning to experience life lessons. In kindergarten, there was no homework, but we still got practice problems. Those days really were the introduction to what school would be like in the future.

Growing up was a delight despite its small crises. Since Neill and Lara competed in so many skating events, I got to travel with them and my parents to what seemed exotic destinations. We traveled to Colorado, Chicago, Cape Cod, and Delaware, more locations than I can name. Because of all our travels, I grew to be comfortable with riding in airplanes. I enjoyed voyaging weightless through the air, assuming I had all the possible sources of protection. I would watch movies, play games, chat with whoever I was next to, and read. However, all that certainly changed in a split second on a flight we took when I was about six. Suddenly, there was a bang! The lights went out, and the plane shook. No one seemed to know what might have created this turbulence. All the passengers suddenly fell silent, and I thought we were about to die. In those moments, we were all terrified. Immediately, Mom pulled out the deck of cards, and we played "War" to focus on something else. After a few minutes, the lights came back on, and the flight attendant attempted to calm us all down, informing us that nothing was wrong with the engine but that one of the plane's wings had been struck by a bolt of lightning. That narrowly averted disaster was my first intimation of a downside to the pleasure of flying, my first experience of an event that could have been earth-shattering for all of us.

As the youngest in our family, I had been introduced to so many things I wanted to do that I didn't know where to start. I thought of my basic skills skating lessons at Babson Skating Center as a way to begin following Neill and Lara's path, especially as my coach, Karen Lambert, was the person who had suggested the idea of pairing Neill and Lara. Of course, since I was constantly at the rink, my desire to participate in the activity only increased. The beauty of movement and speed as everybody glided across the ice enchanted me, not to mention that all the choreography looked thrilling. Unfortunately, I couldn't yet do all the jumps and spins I saw Neill, Lara, and their friends did. At first I didn't understand that "Basic Skills" literally meant basic skills. Slowly and steadily the girls in my class learned three turns, bunny hops, and shoot the ducks. I was anxious to succeed at these basic steps so as to move on to the more complex ones. Nonetheless, I was still trying to figure out what interested me most since there were so many different things I wanted to try at that age. I vacillated about continuing to skate and dance ballet, some days saying I loved them, other days wanting to do something else with my time. In the end, however, I would always return to them.

When I was still very young, Neill and Lara stepped up from just skating singles to skating together as a pairs team. They really became a pairs team by accident when the coach, Karen Lambert, thought it would be cute to have them skate together in one of the upcoming shows. Well, that was the simple thought at first, but they soon morphed into a dedicated, committed, and competitive team, competing as both singles and pairs. Their first official pairs coaches were a couple that we all knew well, Karen's daughter, Melanie, and her skating partner, Fred Palestack. Since we now spent so much more time at the rink, I even started skating a little more. This new arrangement also reenforced my status as the "Rink Rat."

Similarly, since Neill and Lara took classes at my mom's ballet studio in addition to skating, my heart was led to that commitment as well. Often I went to the studio when my mom taught. I usually sat in the waiting room drawing pictures. However, when my pre-ballet class appeared in the studio's annual demonstration, I was, as mentioned above, always the one in my class waving to my grandparents before exiting the stage. Not one of my finer moments, but still when I see videos of those performances, I laugh as I witness my social butterfly self, making me obvious to the audience. I was always happy being a performer in every way and even known to become a bit excessive and out of control in environments where that was possible.

I advanced in my levels of dance year by year. Since pre-ballet, I had built an alliance with Reagan, another girl in my ballet class. We always got in trouble for chattering when the teacher, Mom, was talking. Eventually, this became such a problem that Mom would regularly separate us, putting a quiet girl named Katie between us to minimize the chatter. This was a functional idea for Mom because my friend and I no longer disrupted her class. Although I would get to talk with Reagan during stretching time, Katie and I also became very close friends because we were constantly next to one another. In fact, that was the start of what has become a lifelong friendship. Friendships aside, I did finally learn a useful lesson about self-discipline from the process.

My family's involvement with the professional ballet company, Dance Prism, led me to yet more studio time. My feelings about being included were divided as they were about figure skating. I would alternate between wanting to continue skating or dancing and preferring to stick to my own things. I was so young then that, of course, my mind always went in a million directions. At some rehearsals, I would lurk behind Dance Prism's dancers, copying them doing, for instance, the huntsmen's dance from *Peter and the Wolf*. Later I also learned from Mom the stories of each ballet—*The Nutcracker*, *Swan Lake*, *Sleeping Beauty*, and others. Throughout my youngest years, I would go to the studio, watch the rehearsals, and when they were prepared, I would watch the final product on stage from the audience. My eyes sparkled as I saw the adult dancers go from dancing in soft shoes on the soles of their feet to going on to pointe, rising onto their toes and balancing so gracefully. I watched and thought to myself, *One day, I'll do that too.*

Life then seemed a little as if it was in a dream sequence to me. Every summer since I can remember, my family and I vacationed at Goose Rocks Beach in Maine for a month, staying in a little cottage that overlooked the ocean. For the adults, it was a place of escape from daily worries; for all of us, it was a blur of swimming, beach walking, playing, and bicycling. I spent hours on the ocean with my boogie board or playing on the sand.

Mom always said Goose Rocks was a place of magic. It was also a place of lifelong friendships. We generally vacationed at the same time as the Barry family. There were three children in their family too—Carolyn, the oldest and around Neill's age; Matt, who was around Lara's age; and Kathleen, around my age. Every year, our families looked forward to coming up to Maine. Kathleen's father had vacationed there when he was young, and so, like us, they regarded returning to Maine as an annual ritual. Lara and Matt became close friends as were Kathleen and me. When they went skim boarding, Kathleen and I would run out to the ocean either to swim or to ride the waves on boogie boards. We never stopped moving.

We also became friendly with a family from Montreal, Canada, Mark and Nicole Houde, their two teenage sons, Francois and Mathieu, and their cousin, Gabriella. For many summers, the Houdes arrived in Maine at about the same time we did, so we had frequent opportunities to be together. Because I was so little, they all enjoyed humoring me. I built an especially strong friendship with Francois, who even taught me the word "delicious." Every time we all ate something together, Francois would look over at me and say something like, "Marina, how does that cookie taste?" His voice would burst with enthusiasm as he asked me such questions

I always looked back at him and cheerfully replied, "Delicious!"

Everybody laughed at that. Though I could not, at such a young age, register everything, could not understand why they all got such a charge out of that, I laughed along anyway. I did have enough awareness to know that I liked seeing everybody happy.

Time went on with all its accomplishments and losses. My grandmother died when I was six. Her death was an immense, traumatizing loss for our family. She had been a World War II navy nurse, stationed on Guam; though she never discussed her horrifying experiences, we could sense the grit and determination of her character. Whenever our parents were working or celebrating an anniversary, Neill, Lara, and I had stayed with our grandparents. It was always a special time because they read a different selection of stories to us, literally provided a change of scenery and a chance to explore other locations, like the Pine Grove in their backyard. The death of my grandmother deprived us of those days and was the first challenging loss of my life.

In that same fall, I also got stung by a bee for the first time. While climbing on the school monkey bars, always an irresistible attraction, I reached out for the next bar, and as I gripped it, my ring finger closed onto the bee's stinger. The sting was excruciating, especially at the age of six. Instantly, I let go of the bar and collapsed onto the ground. I remember screaming and rolling in the wood chips because it was so painful. Another event on the monkey bars was far worse, however. I loved the monkey bars, and often I would hang upside down by my knees which I had done so many times that I was comfortable there; the inverted position felt like the easiest thing. All that changed in one moment. I started laughing because I was having so much fun. Well, when you laugh, muscles relax. My legs gave out, and I landed on the crown of my head. The nurse called my mom, and I was rushed to the hospital. I was so sick that entire day and out of school for the rest of the week. My concussion was another early prophetic example of how easily a small circumstance can go wrong.

In the winter of 2000, Neill and Lara competed in the Junior Nationals for figure skating. That year, the competition conveniently fell over my seventh birthday. The competition was fierce, with skaters from all over the country. Everywhere you looked, you saw determined, focused expressions. It was a true introduction to the world of real life, competitive stress, and the total commitment success would require. Even I could not think of anything else for the few minutes Neill and Lara were skating. I was completely immersed in their performance and the significance of the event. After the competition, there was a competitors' party that I got to go to. It was the night of my birthday, and it was so much fun! There was dancing, karaoke, and, of course, cake for the competitors, which they let me have some of. It was so convenient for my birthday.

Soon thereafter, I entered my first Basic Skills skating competition at our club, the Colonial Figure Skating Club in Boxborough, Massachusetts. Basic skills competitions are different from regular competitions because each group of competitors consists of a maximum number of four skaters so that everyone earns an award.

This format provides both a gentle way of introducing skaters to competitions and the beginning of forming friendships with other competitors.

I thought I would know how to react to competition because of having observed Neill and Lara, but there was much more I had to learn. I knew from watching my siblings compete that some aspects of competitions were aggressive, but I did not understand the reality of all the effort competing took. In my own world, I imagined that the event would automatically go my way because I had skated for years and I was confident in myself. However, when the day of my first competition came around, I learned a very big lesson.

At the rink, I got dressed in Lara's first skating competition dress, and she did my makeup. There were a few hours before my group took the ice. I didn't know any of the girls in my group, but I walked around with my family and our other skating friends. Since I thought I knew exactly what I was getting myself into, I didn't think a lot about it. In the first few years of my life, I had seen so many people, as well as Neill and Lara, skate, and everyone made it look easy. Well, let's say I was eager for what was coming but not fully prepared.

When I took to the ice to skate my program, I felt energy and excitement surge through my body. I skated to the music with a light in my heart. The audience in the rink seemed to disappear as the program went on. I gained speed, energy, and heightened adrenaline. I could feel it pushing, helping me along. I skated well in the beginning, but I got nervous toward the end for my hardest jump, the lutz. Out of my whole program, this was the jump I was least consistent on in practice. I knew if I spent too much time thinking about it, landing it wasn't even an option. I drove my toe-pick into the ice, did a full revolution in the air, and to my astonishment, landed with my blade on the ice. Whenever I landed my lutz in practice, I always had fun with the rest of the program, and so I did this time. The remainder of my program consisted of a lot of intricate footwork, even more speed, and ended with another spin before I hit my ending pose.

I was overjoyed as I left the ice. I ran into my mother's arms with a feeling of sheer accomplishment. My entire family, my two coaches, by then Bobby and Barbie Martin, and all our friends at

Neill and Lara's levels who watched all hugged me and congratulated me on my first competition.

Suddenly, another family came up to me. It was that of Layla Siraj, one of the girls who had competed against me. I was surprised to be approached by one of my competitors since I was new to competing. I knew in such situations people took competitions very seriously. However, Layla was nice, so I didn't feel as intimidated as I had somewhat been before. I was also confident in how I had skated, so I hadn't even considered my place on the podium. I thought it would be really cool to win my first competition, and I wanted to surprise myself. When the results came out, I wasn't even nervous about where I stood because I thought I knew. However, when I looked at them, I didn't see my name on the top of the list. A little surprised, I scanned the list further. I didn't see it second either. I saw my name after in third place. Layla was in second. There were only three of us. Clearly, I was disappointed, but I knew that there would be other competitions in the future. We all got small trophies for awards.

In addition to my skating competition introduction, I competed in two more Basic Skills competitions. The second was in Fitchburg, Massachusetts. I competed against only one other girl. It honestly felt as if it were another practice in which I was having a great run through. After the competition had ended, my family, competitors, their families, and I all waited anxiously for the results. Around twenty minutes later, the judge came up and tacked a sheet of paper onto a wall. The second it was up, we all swarmed around to get the first look. I was the third person to see the lineup. To my delight, my name was first on the list. Just to make sure my eyes weren't playing tricks on me, I blinked a few times. Nope, it was real.

That was not the last Basic Skills competition for me though. Since I had competed in two already, I really started to capture what skaters felt as truly serious competitors. The events that I had competed in thus far didn't have the same level of aggression that bigger competitions over the world, like the Olympics have, but they were a great start to it all. For my third competition, Boston Basic Skills, there were four girls in my group. One was Layla, whom I hadn't seen since our last competition, another girl, and my friend, Alex

Potts, who went to my school. I was a little nervous at there being four people in my group. Up to this point, I had never skated against more than two competitors.

When it was my turn to skate my program, I felt the adrenaline rush as I stepped onto the ice. I felt strong as I glided out into the center of the rink and took my beginning pose. I remember thinking to myself that the audience seemed to disappear as I fell into deep concentration. As I skated my program, I felt the same ease but also determination to get through this in the best way I could. I knew I was up against three other girls this time, but I didn't let that cloud of uncertainty overtake me. I expended the same surges of energy in my jumps, spins, and elements as I had at the beginning. I ended with strength, and I just took a deep breath as I hit my ending pose. I put myself in deep concentration whenever I competed, but I was still aware of what I had done during my skate. I was not completely sure what place I came in until the results appeared, so I enjoyed the cheers and applause from the crowd and used what was left of my energy to really exaggerate my curtsy to them. I was always a little tired after a competition program, so I let myself enjoy the crowd's reactions and, as I often did after skating, collapsed into Mom's arms.

I remember waiting around anxiously again for one of the judges to post the results. That was a pattern overall for competitors. Not knowing our placement was the hardest part. I felt confident about my skate again, so, of course, butterflies kept flying in my stomach. I was especially anxious because I had won the last competition and so was really excited to see the outcome. I kept pacing the floor, looking at my parents and the other competitors.

Finally, a judge came out and tacked up our sheet on the wall. We swarmed over to the sheet like bees going to a hive. We all wanted the first look. When I made it over, I saw my name second on the list. I was a little disappointed that I had not won this time, but I told myself I had done my best and could not possibly win *every* competition. After I reminded myself of all this, my stomach went back to feeling normal. I nodded and grinned because it might not have been what I was looking for, but it was still an accomplishment. I would still stand on the podium and get a medal. When the awards came out and I heard my name called, my face lit up, and I happily stood on the second platform. I still felt a sense of triumph and confidence as we all clapped for each other, and the crowd who came down to support us all cheered. Part of the pleasure, too, came from successfully living up to my brother and sister's example. To this day, I have a photo of Lara putting my makeup on me before I skated in one of the competitions. I don't remember which competition that was from, but I was pleased that it made me feel I was bonding with my big sister before an important experience in which I followed in her footsteps.

A few years later, at the Skating Club of Boston, my family and I met a man named Scott Smith. At the age of twenty-one, he was a senior men's competitor whom we had seen in global competitions like Nationals and Worlds. After we had met a few times at the Skating Club, a powerful friendship between him and our family started to take shape. As time went on, he was at our house more and more. Since he lived in Boston back then, he often came to our house to hang out. He'd even come by on some holidays as well. He and I came to be very close; he felt like a second brother to me. When my family and I went to the World Skating Competition in Washington, DC, we were able to stay with Scott at his home in Sandy Springs, Maryland. Astonishingly, the bedroom I was offered featured a bunk bed. My bed at home was a regular single bed, so, of course, I loved this novelty! It was only me in that room, so I happily claimed the top bunk. I loved staying there, not because of the bunk bed, although admittedly that did have its advantage, but overall, I loved that Scott let us stay with him. It felt like another home away from home.

Since we were already in Maryland, one day we decided to take a side trip to Washington, DC. It was incredible to finally see everything from a personal perspective. The city was so beautiful. Unfortunately, the terrorist attack at the World Trade Center had happened that September, so many national landmarks were guarded. For example, we drove up to see the Pentagon, but we couldn't get very far; we were stopped by guards who wouldn't let us get close, which was very understandable, so we drove around the outside of it instead. We also drove past the White House, which I had wanted to see most of all. I loved the opportunity our skating expeditions gave us to see new and important places.

When I was nine, I also started skating with an ice theater team out of the Skating Club of Boston, which conveniently was only twenty minutes away from my house, about the same travel distance as our usual Colonial facility. Our program was set to segments of the music from *West Side Story*, a modern-day version of the *Romeo and Juliet* tale. The idea is the same, but instead of two families keeping apart the main characters, Tony and Maria, two gangs, more specifically the Sharks and the Jets, separate them. Half of the older skaters were the Jets, the other half the Sharks. The children, skaters of around my age, were also divided into groups allied with the Americans and Puerto Ricans. Many of the principal characters were played by our friends: Simon Shaper as Tony, Chynna Pope as Maria, Robbie Flynn as Bernardo. I was one of the children. For the opening of our program, we were divided into two groups, the Americans and the Puerto Ricans. We all lined up against the boards in each of our sections. Before the music started, a voice from the musical gave a brief synopsis and commentary about our story. The announcer started the musical with these words:

> In a time where we will mistrust one another,
> whether it be because of culture, religion, race,
>   or color.
> How can one know what is right?
> Can we come together without a fight?
> Perhaps we can reflect on a time in life today,
> and watch the children as they play.
> See their joy, their spirit, their fun,
> and trust and respect for everyone.
> Maybe there's a lesson here for us today,
> just like the children show us the way.

The announcer went on to introduce Act One of Skating Club of Boston Theater on Ice, but I wanted to make sure to stress this excerpt from the prologue. I have found that the words used to describe the show are true in life. At some points, people in the world do mistrust one another because of the categories noted in these lines, and we don't always know what is right. There really are some instances where we don't know if a matter can be resolved without a fight, without the wars and terrorist attacks. I believe that our lives can be peaceful if we look to the simplicity of life. We could see the simplicity and enjoy happiness and acceptance for all people. The opening speech ends with the familiar idea that we could learn a lesson about life if we took the time to see it through the eyes of the innocent. It reminds us that everybody wants to live a peaceful life, putting into words what most people strive for. At least it captures exactly the way I've always wanted to live.

Our program began with the characters Tony and Maria (played by our friends Simon and Chynna) skating together. Then the two groups skated out in opposite directions. Everyone skated on their own side, the Americans who wore black costumes and the Puerto Ricans who were in white. The children in both groups were playing separately on each side. My group had a Hula-Hoop that we were passing to each other by sliding it on the ice. I was lucky enough to get the opportunity of jumping through the hoop. Miraculously, I don't think I ever fell skating the program in competition, which was always a good thing. The scene went on with Simon and Chynna skating more together, but suddenly, Bernardo (skated by our friend Robbie Flynn) darted out and tore them apart. Then the fight started. The older skaters all grabbed the children and skated backward with us so that we were out of the way. For about half a minute, Simon and Robbie portrayed a false fight until one of the children, my friend Melody, stopped it. The program ended with everyone coming together again and becoming integrated as one.

I had the opportunity to skate this program with the full group three times. Our first competition was the Green Mountain Open in Burlington, Vermont. This time I went with my mom. It was a great mother-daughter experience. We drove all the way from our home in Wayland. The whole team stayed in the same hotel, practicing during the day and hanging out in the hotel at night. One evening my mom and I had gone down to the lobby after watching a movie in our room and were pleasantly surprised to find a platter set out with chocolate chip cookies, which were still fresh out of the oven, and a pitcher of milk. We sat there for a little while chomping on warm decadent cookies and washing them down with sweet, creamy, cold milk. It was a great way to experience the life of big-time competitions and traveling.

It was late March, actually a few weeks after my birthday, but still felt like the middle of winter. The air was still cold enough for you to see your breath and to need a big coat when you went outside. Mom and I took a walk around Burlington to familiarize ourselves with the surroundings. As we meandered around, we saw how beautiful the environment looked. The outside was still covered with snow from the snowfall the night before. Other people, too, were walking about with friends and family in winter gear. We ventured out to see Lake Champlain frozen over. There were many people walking on the ice, and some people were even ice fishing. Drawn by what we saw, my mom and I stepped out onto the ice. Now it took a little getting used to because our boots were rubber. The only way I was used to being upright on ice was on skate blades. After a few minutes of slipping and sliding, my mom and I finally held our ground. There was a crisp winter breeze, and we really enjoyed this experience of being on a body of water so well-known. What was especially surprising to me was to see the enormous number of people who were on the lake as well.

During the competition the next day, everything went successfully. We skated against one other theater on ice team, the Bluebirds. When we all took the ice after they finished, I remember thinking to myself, *Okay, we can do this. It was time to put what we had practiced every week for months to work for us.*

The music started, and our nerves seemed to evaporate. We skated the program confidently and memorably. Honestly, it felt as if it was just another practice, but a really great one. None of us were jumpy or out of alignment. I always loved the feeling of moving so smoothly that I forgot about the competition for a moment, and suddenly, it felt as if there was no one else left on the ice or in the rink. We skated our program energetically with a lot of appropriate emotion. It was clear that we had trained rigorously all the weeks leading up to this first traveling competition. Our program told the story exactly the way it was portrayed in the musical even though some things had to be condensed for the sake of time. The magical feeling of unity and commitment we experienced helped us to skate a high-quality program.

After the competition had ended, my team and I excitedly awaited the results. We felt confident about our program and were anxious to see what the judges thought of it. Finally, one of the judges posted the results on the wall. Here again, we all dashed over to see. Our hearts sank slightly as we saw our group in second place. We thought the Bluebird team had not even skated like an ice the-ater team; they skated a program more like synchronized skating but seemed to passed it off as theater. To us, it didn't make sense that the other team still beat us, but that's the way competitions work sometimes. We all kept a good attitude about it. We were together as a team, at our first traveling competition, and we skated a clean program as a senior team.

That night, the excitement and energy from the competition had still not worn off. Mom and I walked back to our hotel room after we had eaten, and as we passed the lobby, we noticed that the tray of cookies was missing. We wondered where they were and why the hotel might not have set them out since they had every other night. However, as we were walking past one of the skater's rooms we heard a lot of voices. We knew it was the room Simon and his parents stayed in, and, of course, we are such a curious family, irresistibly drawn to most action, that we felt compelled to knock on the door. As the it opened, we saw the whole team. The tray of cookies had been smuggled into the room, and Simon and Chynna were leading a competitor's party there. I laughed when I saw the tray and thought to myself, *Well, I guess we know now why they were missing in the lobby.*

It was so sneaky that they took the cookies and then got away with it. The whole team was in the room for the party. It was surpris-ing that so many people could fit in a three-person hotel room. Well, of course, we just had to stay. Everyone was so excited, and I was more than happy. We partied until after midnight, all simply mingling, drinking sodas, eating cookies, laughing, and reflecting jubilantly on the competition and our time together. The party seemed as if it might never have stopped, but the fact that everyone on our team had to leave the next morning put a closing time to this fun.

Needless to say, that trip was amazing. My family and I had all traveled to numerous places for Neill and Lara's competitions, but finally traveling outside Massachusetts for one of my own team's competitions made it that much more special. Mom and I got to handle things our own way, and we had some wonderful moments that would never have happened if not for this competition. Through this, we created memories we could hold onto forever. It was such a special time that we hated to leave even though we knew that there would be other opportunities to do trips like this, just Mom and me. Saying goodbyes to the team was hard as well, but we thought about it the same way: there will always be other traveling competitions for all of us to take part in.

My team and I soon skated our second team competition at the Boston Open, an event held at the Skating Club of Boston, which was where we practiced and formulated the program. This competition was a little more comfortable for us because it was at our own skating club; the ice was familiar. We knew where jumps and other elements felt good and could feel confident faster than we would have otherwise. We skated another clean program, and our butterflies subsided as we finished. I think we got second place in that competition as well, up against probably three or four other teams. We all had a sense of pride and accomplishment when we produced a great skate in competition.

Skating competitions were not the only thing Neill, Lara, and I had to train hard for. We all still studied ballet at Mom's studio. As I had emerged from my toddler years, I had finally got up the sense not to wave at people I saw in the audience. That was a step up for me and a big accomplishment. Each year thereafter, I moved up one level, and as these classes became more advanced, they better showed the growth of a dancer. The demonstrations were easier than skating competitions because other dancers and I stood on a stage floor in ballet slippers. Understandably, standing on solid ground was easier than balancing with two blades on ice and moving at the same time. It did not always have the same speed, but that was a good thing in a way because dancers concentrated more on holding their upper body. Now, it can be argued that ballet experience is good for the artistry of skating because posture, grace, and stability are important elements of both art forms, but because of all the technicalities required, I think there are more difficulties in figure skating. Nonetheless, ballet was enjoyable to all of us, as well as functional in the way it assisted us in skating. Incorporating movement into music came naturally to all four of us: my mom, the ballet teacher, Neill and Lara, the pairs skating team, and me—the one who was always at the rink with Mom.

As everything played out, I was very happy with my life. The year 2003 was one of the most crucial years for me. I entered the fourth grade and knew I progressed toward my entrance into middle school. I made strong friendships that year, especially with two girls in my fourth-grade class, Swathi and Michelle. We were three of a kind, always together in class, running around being a bit crazy during recess. We loved being together. When I was with them, I knew I had true friendships at school. At that same time, I absolutely formed a great friendship with my teacher as well. When her birthday came around, I made her a little cake figurine that I had seen in a book and made at home from Sculpey clay, the product of my continuing fascination with the arts and crafts. I was a happy student, and I loved my class.

That same year, I also had made physical strides in skating. After those basic skills competitions, I finally progressed to open competitions as a singles skater. For the first time, I competed against a dozen girls; I used the same program I skated in my Basic Skills. In honor of my growth through competition, my mom allowed me to have my own competition dress made. I was overjoyed and already envisioned what I wanted the design for the dress to be. It was a long dark purple dress with bell sleeves, and the ends of the skirt and the sleeves were layered with bright pink, bright turquoise, and orange fabrics. I still have it even to this day.

I have a funny memory of the first day I went with my mom to the skating dress designer for a fitting. I had drawn the design I wanted with the sleeves three-fourth length. When we saw it in the store, it had long sleeves. My mom laughed because she saw the expression on my face and knew what I was thinking, but I said nothing and took it into the dressing room. Now I really thought it was a beautiful dress, and I was happy with what the designer did. After I had it on, I came out of the dressing room, and my mom burst out into uncontrollable laughter. I had taken the sleeves of the dress and pulled them up to my elbows. After I walked out, the designer looked at me and said, "Oh yeah, it looks nice with sleeves that length." She kept the dress for about a week so that the sleeves could be fixed and some other adjustments could be made. When I went in and tried it on for the second time, I thought it was one of the most beautiful skating dresses I had ever seen. It was exactly the way I imagined it. The fit was perfect, and I loved the way the layers at my elbows bounced beautifully halfway up my arms as I moved my hands over my head. The skirt was short so as not to catch the skater's blades, but the three short layers moved every way my waist moved. When I first exited the dressing room, I spun around so the layers of the skirt moved with the air, and you easily saw how each layer of the fabric fanned out. All three of us, my mom, the designer, and I, were awed by its beauty. There were three flowers of the same colors sewn on under the collar of my dress. Each was a big pink flower, with a purple flower within that, and a smaller turquoise one within that. What made it even more beautiful were all the rhinestones. The end of each pink flower petal was adorned with a rhinestone. Two green fabric leaves, each with three tiny green rhinestones, separated each flower from the next. I love sparkles. Those stones made the dress twinkle every which way I moved. It caught the light quite easily and moved with grace—just like me. It was even prettier than the dress I had imagined.

Fast-forward a few months to the day of the competition. I proudly wore my competition dress. I looked out at the ice before my warm-up as butterflies fluttered uncontrollably in my stomach and my heart beat fast. I saw the other girls who were in my group out before me. I felt the adrenaline as it rushed through me. Mom had done my hair and makeup earlier but saw me standing at the base of the ice and came to my side.

"Oh, a lot of these girls have axels, and I haven't even gotten mine yet," I said.

I had worked on my axel jump all that year, but I hadn't landed it cleanly yet. At that moment, I grew even more nervous because I knew I was up against girls who had a physical advantage over me. An axel is a jump in which skaters jump into the air, do a full rotation and a half, and land on one foot. I had gotten to the level where I jumped and got the full rotations, but I always double-footed the landing. Still I knew for the competition, I needed to focus on what I was capable of skating cleanly, and that would be an accomplishment. It would also build my confidence for future competitions. I simply reminded myself that I had practiced technical aspects constantly, I had a positive attitude about my first competition, and wherever I ended up, there would be more competitions in my future.

My heart thumped as I went on to the ice. Before my name was announced, I warmed up a jump with my coach. A minute later, everybody in the rink heard the announcer's voice over the loud-speaker, "Representing the Colonial Skating Club of Boxborough, Massachusetts, please welcome, Marina Shelton."

There was an eruption of applause from the audience as I skated out. I went into the center of the ice with a bright smile on my face and took my opening position. Despite the way my heart thumped, I knew I was ready. When the upbeat music began, I followed every beat. I moved quickly to the speed of it, and as I entered my first jump, I had a positive feeling about how the rest of my program would be. I did a mohawk, stuck my toe pick into the ice, flew up in the air, did one rotation, and landed cleanly on my blade. I skated the rest of my routine with immense energy. The amount of fun I had in this program was evident. My program had several other jumps, spins, and elements that I was proud of. However, I was unsure of what the outcome would be of one element toward the end—my lutz jump. As it was one of my last jumps and specifically the one I had always had the most trouble with, I understood that it was crucial to my placement.

I knew I couldn't let my worries distract me, especially at that moment. I did some back crossovers, brought my leg behind me, tapped my toe pick into the ice, jumped into the air, did one full rotation, and landed cleanly on one blade. It felt as if a huge weight had been lifted off my shoulders after that. The moment I landed, my smile widened. I skated the rest of my program with even more speed and enthusiasm. I had choreographed a portion of one section in which I ran on both toe picks and brought my arms up. This time, I ran quickly on my toe picks with a bright smile and clapped my hands together over my head. I did a split jump, several other jumps, and ended with a layback spin, finishing as the last note of music played. I was overjoyed with my program; it was clean, and I had landed my lutz perfectly. I felt great about how I had skated, but in the back of my mind, I knew the competition was far from over.

I watched the other skaters through the end of my competition, still a little nervous because of what I had seen from my opponents during our warm-up. Among my competitors this time were my friends, Layla and Alex; it was always fun to compete against friends but also a little nerve-racking because I didn't want placement to affect our friendship. Thankfully, it never did. After all the girls in our competition finished skating, we awaited the judges' results. One of the much anticipated judges came out after about twenty minutes and tacked a piece of paper to the wall. The competitors and I all swarmed around the sheet of paper, still like honey bees at a beehive.

I squeezed in with a group of other girls who also were anxious about our outcome. I finally got a glimpse of the sheet and walked closer to get a better look. A surge of emotions went through me as I saw my name at number five. I was disappointed I had not medaled, but I only missed that by one placement, and I was happy with being placed above more than half of the skaters who at the beginning of the competition I had thought were so much better than me. Layla had gotten fourth, ahead of me by one placement again. Oh, well. As a good teammate, I walked over and congratulated her. I had seen her program as she took the ice right after I finished. She skated beautifully. Then I went to congratulate Alex, my friend from school, and gave her a hug.

After my part of the competition, my family and I all stayed a few hours to watch our other friends as they competed. There was always an extra magic that came from observing others. As each person skated, you somehow seemed to understand or learn how a jump or other element could be fixed as observers compared how each succeeding skaters took off for it. Before heading home, we went out to dinner as a celebration of the fact that I had done my first bigger skating competition.

My ballet life continued to develop in parallel to skating. My entire family performed in *The Nutcracker* with Dance Prism every fall and winter. I started dancing in it when I was very young, and my friend Katie was soon involved as well.

Growing up as a performer in a performing family was fun and also helped to make me who I am. We were in the unusual position of being able to engage in these annual productions all together, as a family, like how we did with skating. Mom always played Clara's grandmother, but she had performed other roles, such as Flowers and Marzipan, in the past. Neill was the Nutcracker Prince for several years, and Lara performed nearly all the girl's roles over time. My dad couldn't exactly fit in that category as much because of his work, but he played a Party Parent. He was surrounded by performers and sometimes danced with my mom for fun as well. (He also ran the music every year for Mom's ballet demo.) Over the years, I moved from Caroler to Mini Doll and Page and then to Reindeer and Soldier in the production. Growing up with the challenge and responsibility, as well as the playfulness, of these roles I think contributed to creating my unique, individual personality.

Part of the pleasure of being in *The Nutcracker* also related to the friendships that evolved among the dancers. Katie and I danced in the same roles every year, so we were together a lot. We were also very friendly with a girl named Melanie, who has remained my friend throughout my life. Often, in between shows, dancers sat together around homework or games of cards or in conversation as we all caught up with one another about our year. Many of the dancers never saw each other during the rest of the year because they lived so far apart. Katie and I were together frequently because we lived in the same town, but Melanie, for instance, lived much farther away. *The Nutcracker*, in this sense, was like a reunion for each of us. We saw each other annually, and we spent numerous hours together through rehearsals and shows.

Through our early mornings and late nights leading up to the shows, there was never a quiet moment. Naturally, when performance time came, we always felt the jolts of excitement, the churning in our stomachs, and the craziness as we all scrambled around to get ready. At about an hour before a performance, our internal lights switched to the "everybody panic" moment. It was nerve-racking to look back at the stage through the closed-circuit TVs and see everything going on. As soon as we realized the time, everybody sorted through costumes, makeup, and props, and altogether we rushed to get everything in proper order.

The shows were always a blast to do and memorable to finish. Through each performance, we could feel the magic of the story coming to life. One minute you were yourself, and then the next minute you had morphed into a character from Christmas Eve of 1892. It was so much fun to become either a Christmas toy, an animal, or a character. Every year after the final *The Nutcracker* performance, all the younger dancers, including the ones in the ensemble, gathered together in a big room for the director to speak about our season together and give some special recognitions. After the speeches, we partied for hours. Everybody mingled together as we all signed each other's annual *The Nutcracker* yearbooks. There was always a blend of excitement as everyone hung out together but also sadness because most of us were not going to see each other until the next year. After the gathering, my parents, some of our friends, Neill, Lara, and I would all go out to dinner. It was the perfect way to celebrate our long season of performances. We all caught up with each other and reflected on what was happening in our lives, having wonderful conversations. These performing experiences that I was able to share with my family and close friends were another huge factor in making me who I am today.

Throughout my first ten years, I constantly saw people doing these tremendous things—ballet performances, skating competitions, plays—and I looked at them wondering how was I ever going to be as good as they were. Of course, doubts would hit me sometimes, but an optimistic attitude kept them from holding me back. Rather, I watched and learned all I could, absorbing snippets of whatever I saw and attempting to apply them to my own movements.

I was in such a happy place with friends, school, skating, ballet, and everything that occupied my life that I felt like the luckiest girl in the world. My life was perfect, or so it seemed. Little did I know I was about to have my life changed forever.

3

SUDDENLY

After my first open competition as a singles skater, everything flowed more smoothly in my life. School became a little harder, but I knew that meant my friends at Loker Elementary School and I only improved. That said, there were some instances where things flowed up and down.

The evening two nights before Easter in 2003, was much like any other. My family and I set things up for the coming holiday, and my brother's friend, Scott Smith, came to visit. We all spent a night typical of the evening before a holiday. We laughed and had a wonderful time together. My family had bought a Nintendo game set many years back, and the bigger the group in our house, the more fun we had. That night, we all sat in our family room and played Super Smash Brothers, a game that combined characters from various other games. There was Mario from Mario 64, Link from Zelda, Pikachu from Pokémon, and many others. As the name Smash Brothers suggests, it was a big fighting game, and the players controlled the characters. Usually, I was not a master at this game, but that night I was on a roll and won many of the rounds. We all laughed when various catastrophes happened, like when someone's character got severely bludgeoned or randomly fell off whatever location we fought on. We all found these instances hysterical because we knew it was only a game. After a grand evening, I was pumped up for the next day.

When the sun rose again, we all had a busy day ahead of us. Scott had gone home but would be back the following evening to get ready for the celebration of Easter with us. For all of us, it was like running a marathon. Many things needed to be done for the next day, and in general, Saturdays were busy enough anyway. I had my skating lesson, a horseback riding lesson, and then finally a rehearsal with my ballet class for Mom's demo. I had a rush of excitement in my stomach because I loved when we prepared for holidays, particularly when we decorated Easter eggs, which we'd do after I went riding. There was also a special Easter vigil mass that night that I had really wanted us all to attend, and that was the plan. Neill, Lara, and I all went up to the rink for a skating session. Saturdays were always crowded there, and that day, the ice was packed with single and pairs skaters. Nonetheless, all three of us took to the ice. Even though it was so crowded, the skaters all easily stayed out of each other's way and found safe spots. It was at least an hour-long session, so all the skaters ran their programs a few times. Neill and Lara, serious pairs skaters by then, did a few runs and then took some time with lifts. I loved whenever there was an opportunity for me, and each time I skated my program, energy and joy filled me.

When the session ended, we all exited the ice. My dad was there before I was done so he could take me to my riding lesson and then a ballet rehearsal in the evening. Lara and Neill either stayed for another session or spent a little time practicing some off-ice pairs lifts. Before I changed into regular clothes and sneakers, I talked to my dad for a minute. I was overjoyed with what he told me. I saw Lara after she left the ice. I ran past her in my skates and announced enthusiastically that Dad had surprised me with a special horseback riding lesson.

I was so excited that I changed quickly out of my lace-sleeved turquoise skating dress and into my riding gear, including the pair of official riding boots I had received as a gift for my birthday a few weeks earlier. I wiped off the blades of my skates with a towel, folded my tights in addition to my dress, and placed them quickly into my large pink skating bag.

Dad and I drove to Bobby's Ranch, which conveniently was not too far from the rink, deep in the woods in Acton. That ranch had an interesting setup; at least it was different from the way I thought most ranches looked. Instead of using a singular big building, they kept their horses in a stable, and there was a separate ring in the barn. Whenever any of us came for a lesson, we either selected a specific horse if there was a one we favored or took any horse that was left in the stable, whether or not we had ridden it before. Most of the time, my first pick was a horse named Cinnamon Bun. She might not have been everyone's favorite, but her gentleness drew me to her. I felt the most comfortable with her and sensed that she knew me.

During the lesson that day, we all rode along the trail and smelled the warm fresh air and brushed the new leaves hanging down from the trees. It felt incredible to be on a horse. We moved as a group, and I felt true happiness. Suddenly, however, there was an abrupt change. I must have felt something bump Cinnamon Bun in her hindquarters. She was alarmed. I did not think she knew what she was doing, but she kicked back, throwing me off. In the instant between the saddle and the ground, I was scared to death, but as soon as I hit the ground, I immediately fell unconscious. The instructor did not know anything was wrong until he heard me scream and turned around. Cinnamon Bun dashed away as if she were in a race. To make matters worse, one of my ankles was still caught in a stirrup. She ran at top speed and, because I was still attached, dragged me behind her. Even today I can't imagine the feelings of horror the girls in the lesson and our instructor must have felt at that moment. The level of fear must have been enormous.

The event was so traumatic that it all seemed surreal. When our riding instructor finally found me, I was completely unconscious, motionless on the ground. Thankfully, he had his cell phone with him, and when he reached me, he instantly called 911. Meanwhile, back in the parking lot of the ranch, Dad waited patiently in the car, as was our post-riding routine, to take me to my ballet rehearsal, which was supposed to follow. Suddenly, he heard a knock on the car window. He looked over and was astounded when he saw a police officer. Dad rolled down the window, and the officer said that he needed to follow them. They walked into the woods, and he saw an ambulance, groups of paramedics, and to his astonishment, me. The first thing he wanted to do was run over and see how bad the damage truly was, but as he started toward me, horrified, the police officer told him that he needed to stay back so that they could attend to me properly. I have never asked Dad what that was like for him. It had to be the most frightening sight he could have had to witness. His younger daughter hurt, and it seemed as if there was nothing he could do.

The paramedics told him that they needed to work as fast as possible in hopes of saving me. They intubated me but had a hard time with the process because even though I was unconscious, some part of me was aware enough that I resisted them. After they struggled for a few minutes, the tube finally went down my throat. They worked quickly to save me without a minute to be wasted. They cut everything I was wearing off me, even a special gold necklace with charms of a figure skate and a pair of pointe shoes. I had just received it for my birthday, and what made it so special to me was that Lara had the exact same necklace. Our two necklaces symbolized our identities as skaters and dancers, but ominously, mine was cut off me. The paramedics loaded me into an ambulance, which drove out of the woods to where a helicopter was stationed, a waiting Medflight helicopter. Thankfully, they were stationed near Acton as every second mattered. Meanwhile, Dad called Mom with the news no mother wants to hear, let alone about her own child. When she picked up, she told him she had my ballet leotard and slippers for me to change into when I got there. She was interrupted by my Dad's still shocked voice as he told her, "There's been an accident."

After those words, I am told, everything seemed to be in a blur for my whole family. Neill and Lara had continued skating while I was at my riding lesson. When they found out, normal life became a hurricane of unimaginable chaos for them. Both were in a state of shock. Neill drove Lara and himself to Boston Medical Center. I wish I could have comforted them, but I could not even wake up. When everyone gathered in the hospital room, their experience was surreal. My accident was a living nightmare for all of us, though in a very particular way for me.

Days in the hospital felt like an eternity for my family. Mom looked for encouragement from the head neurosurgeon, but all he told my family was how injured I was. Neill and Lara still had to go to school and skate for hours in the evening. They endured the pain of seeing my condition at the hospital and then facing questions at school from friends. There was essentially no escape for them.

It was an unnerving experience for everyone. Those first three weeks in the hospital were worse than any of them ever imagined. Just when they thought things couldn't get any worse, they did. One minute I seemed stable, and then the next, my monitors went off, my breathing tube attached to the respirator had to be cleared, and emergency CAT scan runs were required; I was constantly run down for emergency surgery. I had dangerously high blood pressure, my heart muscle thickened, one of my lungs collapsed, and at one point, there were several complications stemming from one of my IVs. I had tubes attached to my body everywhere for food, medicine, blood, and oxygen, measuring everything conceivable. At one point, a nurse had placed into the top of my left foot an IV containing an anti-seizure medicine, Dilantin—not good. It was left there, and to make matters worse, it infiltrated and burned through my skin. Once again, I was rushed into emergency surgery, this time for a skin graft. I needed five of those done because my body each time rejected any other skin used over the open wound. The fifth time this surgery was performed, the doctors took my own skin from my left thigh in hopes that this would help my body heal. Lo and behold, my own skin stayed on.

Other events were similarly horrendous. On one crucial day, part of the medical team, of course, wanted to see if my survival could be sustained without the respirator, but other doctors all thought that was too much of a risk and feared I would have to be trached. The doctor who was head of pediatric surgery confidently declared, "I think she will soar."

That was enough confidence my parents needed especially from the man in charge. They took me off the respirator, but they kept the tools to perform the tracheotomy procedure right away if I needed it. They kept me under watchful eye, but just like he thought, I was able to breathe on my own.

Days passed, and some other patients woke up from their comas, but not much changed with me; I still seemed stuck. Other parents knew my family's pain, spoke with attempted encouragement, but my situation seemed incomprehensible for everyone. Often, friends asked to come see me or do something for my family, but no one wanted to expose too many people to the suffering the family was enduring. Close friends sometimes came as emotional support or came and cried with the family. Bobby's Ranch called frequently because the event was so horrible. The priests from our church back home came into the hospital frequently, offering spirituality and prayers to God for me.

In these impossibly hard times, medicine and prayers seemed to offer the only constant sense of hope to lean on. Of course, none of us foresaw what these events could do before they crashed down upon all of us. There is no way to be properly prepared for sudden disasters such as the one my family experienced, but even when things seemed at their worst, they held on to a faded glimmer of hope.

Some weeks after the accident when Mom came to see me, she encountered a huge surprise. She walked into my room to see my grandfather and my dad leaning over my bed. She looked around their shoulders and was astounded at what she saw. My eyes were slightly cracked open; it was shocking in the best way to everyone involved. At first, all were overjoyed about this new improvement, but then the harsh reality set in. My family was constantly told that I might always be in a semiconscious state, unable to interact, never able to learn past the fourth-grade level, and that I was awake but still not fully conscious. For all of them, it was terrifying to imagine how I would be once I moved home, especially imagining how I might be then compared to the way I was in my life before.

Luckily, however, I had reached a stable point in my recovery and was transferred to Spaulding Rehabilitation Hospital in Boston, which at the time was attached to Massachusetts Eye and Ear Infirmary. Here things seemed a little like Boston Medical Center but better. I was still on many medicines, but my communication ability slowly but surely improved. My first communication tool was a buzzer I pressed for yes or no. The doctors had requested that, as a next step, my parents bring in some toys that responded with a power switch. Thinking of that, Mom remembered that I had been given a battery-powered toy cat for Christmas. She located it at home and curiously turned it on to make sure it was still functional. At that time, our family's pet was retired racing greyhound who was lying peacefully on the rug. The moment the cat was switched on, it meowed and moved its head and tail. Instantly the dog freaked out and bolted into the next room.

The way I fully came out of my coma really created a wonderful memory. At this time, my parents often switched off who stayed with me and who stayed home with Neill and Lara. One day when Mom came to stay with me, she told me the story of the greyhound and the toy cat. As I mentioned earlier, my doctors had warned that I might stay permanently in a semiconscious state, and I was still clearly comatose, so she had not expected a big response. That, however, was exactly what she got. I immediately burst out into an eruption of laughter. That was the thing that actually snapped me out of my state and an instant nobody in my family or I will ever forget. After word got out about this occurrence, people came to see me, always telling jokes. The detail that entertained my parents the most about this was that I laughed at the good jokes but not the bad ones. My fourth-grade class learned about how I woke up thanks to a joke, so the whole class made me a big get well soon card which had many jokes my friends had learned or created and had written inside. On the front of the card was a photo of two of my best friends, as well as a miniature stuffed unicorn taped on by someone who knew I had a reputation for my love of unicorns; it was nice that they contributed that as well. It was wonderful later to realize that so many people were supporting me even though I wasn't aware of them.

At times like these, people need as much faith as possible. Weekly, the priests from the church my parents and I belonged to came into my room. They always visited with me and then said a prayer with us in my room. It was nice whenever they came in because, of course, I had questions. I wanted to know why it happened (which no one really knew the answer to). I asked for help from God, reassurance that improvement was possible, and knowledge that there really was something bigger somewhere out there that guided me through every day.

4

BEGINNING MY JOURNEY

My doctor was right. It was great that I had survived, but the improvements I had yet to make only became more difficult to handle emotionally as I understood how much harder I'd have to work to make the improvements that I wanted. Laughter had brought me out of my comatose state; later, my laughter formed into other noises, and those formed into words. One day, another of my doctors, who had not been informed of the laughter outburst episode came to see me and said hi to me as he did even when I was still comatose.

"Hi," I replied. My voice was still soft since I had just started to get used to speaking again, but he stepped back in surprise and bewilderment. After the amount of energy and persistence they had invested in me, this outcome still seemed unlikely. Some hospitals were so used to having patients that rarely survived the sort of trauma I had that it was thoroughly amazing when they saw one through their entire journey. The difference in patients' improvement resulted from the hard work and hope of their medical professionals. It really is amazing how surprised people are after they have seen someone in one very limited way for such a long time and then see how much progress they had made after time.

When my brain was still slowly waking up, I listened to music and was aware enough to find some enjoyment in it. I was still only partially awake, and I had not reached full communication. My communication was usually a nod or shake of the head for "yes" or "no." However, this day was different. The actor Adam Sandler was visiting his father, who was a patient at Mass General, to which Spaulding was attached. Of course, as he was a famous movie star, the Spaulding ward asked him to come back afterward to visit the patients on the Spaulding side.

About an hour later, he came back to the pediatric ward. He stopped in my room at some point, walked in, and greeted me. I had been watching *West Side Story*, and my mom paused it while he came in. My eyes were still on the TV, and I gave a soft "hi" back. While he was first in my room and a little unsure of what to say, he looked around my room and tried to think about how to associate with me. He then noticed the screen on the hospital TV.

"So what are you watching on TV?" he asked to have something to talk about.

Still with my eyes on the screen, I softly replied, "*West Side Story.*"

He then switched from unsure to beyond excited and said, "*West Side Story*? Oh, I love that movie! I used to watch that with my mom when I was a kid!"

The setting then transformed from my hospital room in Spaulding to 1961 in New York City. Adam Sandler sang the first verse of "A Boy Like That," quoting Anita's lines perfectly. My mom watched us and just smiled because she knew what was coming. The minute Anita's verse ended, my head turned, my arm went out to him, and I sang Maria's exact verse as they followed Anita's. He was shocked that I was interacting this way and that I knew the song so well. We then morphed from "A Boy Like That," which came after Anita's realization of Maria's relationship with Tony, and sang "America," which followed the dance scene in the musical. After a little of that song, we went into "I Feel Pretty," which came during the bridal shop scene the day after the rumble between the Jets and Sharks. We had gone into our own little world for about ten minutes as my mom, doctor, and nurses watched in amazement.

After we had gone into our ten-minute world, he sat down bewildered.

"Wow," he said in disbelief. He then turned to Mom and asked, "What happened to her?"

Mom smiled and, because of the recent events, told him evenly, "She had a horseback riding accident."

Still amazed at my reaction at the same time understanding the situation, he replied sorrowfully, "I hope she gets better."

Mom smiled, looked at him, and said, "Thank you. I hope your dad gets better."

He thanked her and then left to visit the other patients on the ward, but I bet our experience together never left his memory. I don't remember it as much because it happened before I completely woke up, but Mom, the hospital staff, and my physiatrist at the time have always remembered it.

A few weeks later, it was as if things finally started falling into place. I was finally fully aware of things. I ate some foods, but they needed to be pureed because the muscles in my throat were so weak. I also had a feeding tube in my stomach for water. Fast-forward and I was well enough for therapy appointments throughout the day. My fluids still had to be thickened so that they were swallowed properly (clear fluids made me choke), but I graduated from pureed food to soft solid food. That was a very big step for me because it was easier to get solid food than the food that had to be pureed. My family enjoyed it whenever they took me out of my room and went down to the cafeteria or when they brought extra food for me.

As time went on, I improved more and more. I became more social and interactive in my therapies and with my family. Frequently, friends from school visited, also my grandfather, my siblings Neill and Lara, my aunts; I was never alone, someone always stayed with me. My parents traded off days they spent at the hospital. Some days Mom stayed with me while Dad was home with Neill and Lara, and then they switched off. It was hard as I watched them leave because I was never home. Whenever people came in to the hospital, there was almost always a moment when I forgot the seriousness of my situation and felt things were not so different because I saw friends and family again.

My fourth-grade teacher, Ms. Cohen, came in a lot, and she had no qualms as she convinced my parents to leave so that we had time to ourselves. She always painted my nails and read to me. Sometimes, she also brought chocolate bars or truffles. This was perfect because this was another substance my medicine could be hidden in to help alleviate its flavor. It was always incredible to see her. I loved it whenever I saw her or my friends.

One day, she came in early and brought a book called *The Fairy's Gift*. It had been another busy day for me, and my mom stayed at the hospital. That night, Mom read this book to me, and I cried. Another day, I saw a picture that my friend Annie from Loker, my elementary school, had drawn for me with a brief note she had written. The picture was a sailboat called *The Buddy*, and she had drawn the two of us on it. That was another hard hit for me and another indication to me that I had gone through something unimaginable. I asked Mom what she thought made my friend draw that picture and write the note on it. Mom said, "You had an accident."

Finally understanding and realization fully hit me, I started crying. It was also evidence that my emotional responses started to come back, and I finally realized that something horrible had happened to me.

Nevertheless, I persisted. Day by day, my physical abilities improved even more. I used a stander in physical therapy as I needed to regain an upright position memory, and I walked on parallel bars. Still, I wanted nothing more than to be discharged and be home again. I also learned that Travis and his family all folded paper cranes for me. He and I both believe they helped. As time went on, I built connections and friendships with my physical, occupational, speech, and child life therapists. The hospital was close to a mall, so every week the hospital took the patients on outings. Some were to the mall, movies, bowling, ice cream, Plaster Fun Time, and other social places. It was nice when we were out of the hospital even if it was just for the change of scenery.

At the same time I started going on outings with the hospital, I started going on some home visits too. These were usually trips home for a dinner with my family before I went back to Spaulding. Mom even took me back to the studio on occasion. The first time I went back, she pushed my wheelchair into the building, and I said, "I haven't smelled this smell in a long time!"

This was wonderful because I recognized something after I was far apart from it for so long. I also saw the two dance studio again. I remembered both so well that I pictured the two of them even before I went in. I saw the pictures of myself from previous recitals and performances of *The Nutcracker*. I smiled as I took a trip down memory lane. I also recognized my friends who were in the same photos. My heart ached because I had not seen many of them and wondered when I would again. On later occasions, I visited the studio while the girls in my ballet class were there, so I saw them; it was fun, but feelings of missing the past always took over.

One afternoon there, I remembered that my ballet class had prepared a dance to the music "Simple Gifts"; in fact, I was supposed to be at my ballet class to rehearse it directly after my riding lesson on the day of my accident. I asked my family when my class planned to perform it because I wanted to do whatever I could in it. Lara and Mom looked at each other with concern. I knew something was not good after I asked that question. They were silent as they thought about what to say. Mom turned her head back to me and said, "Marina, I rehearsed that piece for the demo last May, and your accident was in April. We already did it. Marina Flessas and I had to choreograph you out of the dance while we were in your hospital room at Boston Medical Center."

This new information silenced me. I had forgotten that time had elapsed and that my class would have already performed that piece. Right then and there, my heart sank, and I burst into tears. I had missed out on another opportunity I had looked forward to. Mom threw her arms around me, emotional too. No one said anything for a few minutes through my sobs. When I finally caught my breath again, Neill and Lara both came over and hugged me. With tears in their eyes, they said, "Marina, we'll do 'Simple Gifts' in the demo with you."

Some days I went back to the studio, and other days I went up to the skating rink with Mom to watch Neill and Lara's practices. Similarly, as I did at the studio, once we drove to the rink, I recognized it, the parking lot, the spot where I learned to read for the first time, and the entire building. Every time I went in, people warmly welcomed me because it had been so long since they had seen me. My coaches and other friends from before I got hurt always came up and said hi to me. Often, I saw Simon who skated there as well, and before my accident, he frequently did pairs lifts with me when we were on the ice together. Frequently, I saw Cameron. He and his mom were always there while his older brother, Drew, trained. My friend Chynna also had come into the hospital and painted my nails. We reminisced about Ice Theater and simply talked.

A few weeks later, it was as if things finally fell into place. I slowly gained more consciousness and started more physical, occupational, and speech therapies. To further my cognitive processes, I joined the other patients in meal groups for breakfast, lunch, and dinner. These were held in a main section of the hospital that was not too far from my room. Every morning, Mom or Dad filled out an order form in my room before we left so that the hospital staff got the orders in advance. It was hectic most days, but it all worked out for the patients. After breakfast group, our day began. I started my day with physical therapy, then occupational, and speech therapies. All the patients got together for a lunch group in the afternoon. We had another break after that and went into the cognitive group where all the patients played games that kept us alert and interactive. We then had dinner group at five, and after that we relaxed. In the mornings, one of the hospital staff came into our rooms and replaced the trash bags. When Mom stayed with me, she always climbed into bed with me, and we pretended we were asleep. Whether he ever believed we were always remained a mystery, but he probably knew.

I also became very close to my nurses. There was a nursing student named Kenndy who often came in and helped with me. We became very close friends. When she first arrived at my room, she helped with me in the shower. Then if I didn't go to the dining room with the other patients, she watched TV with me while I ate breakfast and we prepared for the day ahead. My other nurse, Maria, was friendly and had a very strong connection with me as well. She always talked with me and really formed a connection with my family as well. Every night when my visiting family members left, she held me as I cried.

When I needed more Botox injections so that the tightness loosened up in my left arm, Maria and my other nurses, Josephine, and Darci, even danced into my room to distract me from the needles as they went in. There was also another time where my child life specialist was with me going through an "I Spy" book where we tried to find specific things hidden in the pages. This was both successful and pleasant because it distracted me from the needles going into my arm and thumb, but searching on the pages also made me happy again because it was fun. Unfortunately, this did not happen every time my doctor came in for this reason, but whenever it did, it was worth their effort. Aside from Botox, we always made each other laugh, and I loved knowing my body made improvements.

I was happy to have friends again whom I saw every day even if I was not home. While I was there, I made friends with some of the other patients, especially the teenage girls. One girl became close to my family while I was still comatose. Another girl was not as close to my family, but she bought me a little plastic doll that had clothes that clipped on. When I fully woke up, I became friends with other patients, Bethany, Becky, and Liz. Most of them were in the hospital for a pain management seminar. We loved our time together; we always sat together at meals, went on the various outings as a group, and hung out whenever we got the chance. Unfortunately, they all left within a few months, but I've always cherished the time we had. We met up in Natick years after our hospital time. It was so special to have great friends.

The months went on, and everything seemed slow. My parents and I saw patients as they arrived and left. So many people. It was so frustrating. Still I worked as hard as possible. As days passed, the progress was slow and steady, but it was there. I eventually graduated from my wheelchair to using the standing board, relearning how to be upright. Some days, however, I wondered if I'd ever really be discharged to go back home. I always grudgingly reminded myself, "It'll happen, Marina. It just takes time."

5

FACING THE TRUTH

I improved day by day, but something was never quite right in the back of my mind. I had always been such an enthusiastic and adventurous girl that my life seemed as if nothing bad could happen to me. Clearly, I was wrong, but I wasn't about to let an injury hold me down.

For a while, I was still in denial about my handicap. It was all still very new to me; I had always been told that I would get better in time, and yet in school, I couldn't participate in some activities I loved. I couldn't skate or join my ballet class, and my attention span, while improving, was still not perfect. What was even harder was that sometimes when I went to visit in Spaulding, I would hear about certain patients who were also in wheelchairs when I was there recently had walked in to visit the nurses and therapists. For a while, I didn't let myself see improvements that other people recognized I made because they still weren't the way I wanted them to be. I was still the same perfectionist, and I really wanted things to go back to exactly the way they used to be.

The truth was a lot harder to accept than I had first anticipated. Even with my level of frustration, I still knew that I had a long way to go. That realization genuinely helped me to work; my motivation to overcome my limitations really blossomed. I wasn't happy that I had to face the truth this way, but I do believe that that's what made me stronger and more motivated. Though this truth hurt, it was another flower to add to my bouquet of accomplishments. I thought that since I had proven so many people wrong after waking up from my coma, this would be another thing I'd overcome.

Even from what I already knew about my abilities, I thought it was just a matter of time before everything would be back to normal again. The amount of time was much more than I thought, but as I got stronger each day, I knew I was getting closer and closer to restoring my physical mobility. I knew what I could do at that point but also that I was capable of so much more. I knew as well that there was more work I needed to do. I just didn't think I'd need so much or that it would be so hard for so long. As I approached each day, I watched as people walked around and from that, tried to figure out what I needed to do better. Here I was, like the skater and dancer I had been, measuring their time, quality, quantity, speed, anything I could judge that I needed to improve on.

Facing the truth of my whole new situation was hard on all of us. My family knew me as the one who followed in Neill and Lara's footsteps, wanting to be just like them. My friends knew me as the creative and wild person who always stood up against a challenge. After I was hurt, it was harder to understand, to know where I would stand because of my limitations. I understood how hard it was to walk, but I thought my balance would easily come back. Wherever my mobility was at the time, I did not want to accept that it represented my final improvement. I wouldn't settle for less than my best. If I fell while walking, I just picked myself up, thought about what went wrong, and I judged what could have caused the fall so I knew how it could be completed better.

Accomplishments take a lot of work. Sometimes this is hard to understand because what we do ordinarily seems so easy. Whether we really believe we can realistically achieve whatever it is we want depends on how much time and effort we're willing to put forward. It's never fun to think that something is out of our reach, especially when we have come so close to it. Being the person I am, I know that once we start on our own challenging voyage, we need to persist relentlessly or else we will never reach the end.

One night, I was sitting with Mom, and I just cried. Everything was getting to me: the fact that my learning was so much slower, that I couldn't run around with my friends as I used to, that I still needed Botox shots every few months in my left arm to loosen the spasticity, and that I felt as if I had made everything so much harder for my family. I cried mainly as the realization that things really were different set in.

"Mom, why me? Why did this really happen? I never thought something this bad could happen to me. Why?"

Lara came in too. She looked at me then walked over and soothingly fingered my hair. I knew the whole situation had been extremely hard on her, so she didn't need to say anything. I felt the sister connection just by having her there. Sometimes saying nothing says everything. After a moment of silence, Mom gave the only answer anybody could give. "I don't know."

It felt like a bad dream for a while. I had thought that I would be walking, skating, and dancing in no time. Even in the hardest times, however, I knew I had to stay confident. My confidence really kept me going even though I wasn't happy with my struggles. Obstacles would get in the way, but there was always hope. Once, when I was on a home visit from Spaulding, Lara took me into the living room, turned some music on, got me out of my chair, and we danced for twenty minutes or so. We had a blast together, and it was also therapeutic. It was a wonderful way to have fun, to feel as if I was again doing something I missed, and it was helping my body all at the same time. It gave me that joyful feeling that I had forgotten.

6

OVERWHELMING

Time went on, and still I felt as if I was stuck. It seemed as if every-one else was moving onto different and new things. I didn't want to let what I saw others doing get the best of me, but sometimes these feelings erupted inside of me before I could stop them. Occasionally, I felt as if I was in another nightmare. Still I knew I couldn't give up because then what I had the potential to do would remain a mystery, and I didn't want the hard work I put in to seem like a waste of time. There were a lot of changes I wasn't prepared for. The physical part was the worst, but many other parts of my life, including my learning style, changed as well.

Some of my friendships changed. I had been accustomed to running around with my friends, but suddenly I couldn't do that anymore. Several people to whom I had been close before stopped hanging out with me because I couldn't join in on activities they did. Further, with my home therapies, tutoring, and such, I didn't see a lot of my friends. When I had time, they were usually involved with school, schoolwork, and other activities. Being that as it is, whenever I could, I still invited some of my friends to hang out on weekends. But it was hard not knowing when I'd see people outside of school when we all were so busy with our own things. I understood that they still wanted their own time, and I wanted them to enjoy them-selves, so I tried not to let this bother me.

There were plenty of other things I could do that felt really good. Any time I had trouble with something, I tried doing them other ways. Being at school during gym was at times really overwhelming. At these times, I saw everyone else running around together having a blast. Even as I watched them, however, I knew my options: keep watching them and feeling sorry for myself or throw a ball back and forth with a friend. My gym teacher and most of my friends at least tried to accommodate the games so that I could be included, which felt really good.

Still there were some things that made me really upset. I loved watching Neill and Lara's skating practices, but being a witness to them brought all my own skating memories back. Occasionally, too, I saw my friend and former skating colleague, Layla, and her little sister, Yasmin, with their parents when there were club dinners at the Skating Club of Boston. Being reminded of the difference between the reality of their situation and mine was painful. They could still skate with all the different movements, but I couldn't. In such situations, I tried to hide my distress, but I wouldn't always be able to. Most people could easily tell when I was about to cry.

This also happened when I watched the ballet lessons at Mom's studio. I sometimes attended my old ballet class in the level they were in now. I watched them moving along to what Mom taught them. It was all so beautiful, and it brought back memories of when I was in class with them as well. I knew that I didn't want them to think that I wasn't enjoying their class, so I kept actively watching. I really did enjoy it, so I tried not to think about what I remembered. It was fun to see them but hard as well. I tried to keep my head held high, but sometimes my emotions got the better of me.

There were other things that I didn't want to accept at first. The whole thing seemed surreal. I knew that accidents happened to people, but I never thought that one could happen to me. My whole life, I wanted to do amazing things, but suffering a traumatic brain injury wasn't what I had in mind. For a while it all seemed hopeless because so much had changed for me. I watched people walking around, and sometimes tears ran down my face because I wanted that independence again.

For the longest time, I didn't want to believe what had happened to me or that I had a handicap. I remembered everything I used to do and just wanted all my physical issues to go away. Most people know that the kinds of achievements they want take a lot of work; some people, however, are not prepared for how long their journey of hard work is. I know I wasn't. Repeatedly, it felt like beloved things were slipping away.

Knowing the things, I couldn't do was hard, but each day, I pushed myself further and closer to new abilities. None of these were easy to obtain, but after my daily therapies, weekly pool therapy, working out more with the AccesSportAmerica group at the Brighton YMCA and after school once a week, I knew how much stronger I was getting. If I just focused on the things I could do versus what I couldn't, my life would be much brighter. I still wanted everything to go back to how it was before the accident, but it couldn't without hard work, perseverance, and the emotional frustration needed to keep pushing me along. What I could not do was wait for another miracle.

Therefore, on some Saturdays, I began skating again on the public ice at Skating Club of Boston. I was so excited to get back to skating; I just wasn't prepared for what I was about to find out. When Dad first walked me to the entrance to the ice, I stepped out, put my blade on the surface, and my leg immediately slipped forward. Luckily, Dad had a good grip on me, so he pulled me back before I fell. I put my other foot on the ice, and the same thing happened. Someone was holding my walker, but it was still a struggle for me to get into it and remain standing on the blades. Even when I was in the walker, I still couldn't stand up straight right away. I had skated so much before my accident that having it become so hard for me was earth-shattering.

Luckily, as we made it around the ice a couple of times, I got more comfortable, and it was easier to stay over my skates. It always took some time before my legs stopped sliding in front of me, but eventually it worked out. It was fun to be back, but it was also hard to accept that this really was how it was for me now. I loved how I skated before my accident, and it was so frustrating that I couldn't do jumps or spins anymore. I felt as if my life had changed even more than I had even imagined.

Clearly, I couldn't do everything I used to do, which I understood, but that wasn't going to stop me from trying. I just needed some new perspectives. There were times I broke down, remembering the things I once did and recognizing the things I could no longer do. The ride was clearly going to be bumpier than I thought. I needed to keep my eyes open and be even more open-minded.

One accomplishment I'm most proud of was starting therapeutic horseback riding. After what happened, people thought I'd never get back on a horse. I still loved horses, and after I heard from my physical therapist that it's actually therapeutic and really good for my body, I was thrilled to have a good excuse to ride again. After asking permission a number of times, I even started jumping, which was so much fun. From a therapy angle, horseback riding works trunk control because we use that to balance in the saddle, and it stretches out our hamstrings and hips because our legs are over each side of the horse. I also thought that if I could ride again, it would prove to everyone that I wasn't afraid to face what should have killed me. I believe I got a second chance at life, and I wanted to show others that anything's possible, even when a situation is literally the worst-case scenario. Hurdles aren't fun to have to go over in life, but the best thing about surpassing them is that afterward—people feel so much stronger. Out of everything I have done since my accident, that accomplishment is what I'm most proud of.

People can't be happy all the time. Occasionally, there will be feelings of frustration, sadness, or even loss of hope. This is important to recognize because it is the truth that can help us want to put more effort in so that they can reach their goal. I was glad when I finally started believing this because it simply meant that I didn't have to feel guilty when people saw me get upset about my limitations. Being sad or frustrated doesn't have to be regarded as a negative factor because if we are never sad, we won't try to improve on issues that troubles us. When I first moved home, what I could and couldn't do were tough struggles for me to accept. I was still part of *The Nutcracker* where I spent time with Katie, Melanie, and a new dancer named Tianna. The four of us were like sisters. We were always together, and they included me in every event I'd be able to do with them. We were always laughing together and enjoying each other's company. Even though my ability to dance was limited, being with such close friends brought back memories of my past.

Even when people become really upset and want to give up, they can't or at least shouldn't. No one likes it when a huge goal seems hopeless or out of reach, but challenges are needed to prove our character to ourselves as well as others. They can be understood as an indicator that we must seek other ways of seeing our effort through to the end. There is an answer to most things; it just might mean we must look at the problem through another perspective. This is indeed difficult, especially when what we want seems so out of reach. There isn't a clear answer as to why things happen as they do in the world, but there is a chance they might happen for our benefit in the long run. We all know that nothing is easy at first, and sometimes it's hard to see the light and know that there's hope, no matter what the cost is. Whatever situation we are going through, people need to hold on to the possibility that things will get better.

Many of us still want what we originally desired. It might have seemed like an easy thing to grasp until we started and realized how much more commitment would be involved. Not getting the answer we had wanted can be beyond frustrating. As overwhelmed as we may be with the present situation, we still can't conclude this to be the final answer. In this instance, we can take our frustration and turn it into motivation; that's the perspective from which I try to look at things most of the time. Even the obstacles in the way can trigger us to exert ourselves. As hard as it is to accept what changes we may experience after a disruptive incident, they really can be for the better and maybe even allow us to discover new things that we would have otherwise missed.

If we look around at everything else happening in the world, what we're upset about might not seem as bad. People can also find things they want to overcome while we still can, possibly recognizing diverse ways we can support ourselves or others or even figure out ways we can help communities. This could be as simple as finding a situation that has an ongoing struggle, such as a country with extreme poverty, gathering up some friends, holding meetings, and over a matter of time raising money or sending food that was collected. Engaging in such efforts gives us the sense that we are helping a global struggle, showing the amount we care and seeing an issue through that wouldn't necessarily have the same positive outcome. Doing such things provides us a sense of accomplishment and encourages us in our own struggles.

I couldn't do everything I used to do, which I knew, but that wasn't going to stop me from trying. I just needed some new perspectives. At times I broke down, remembering the things I had done and hearing about the things I now couldn't do. The ride was clearly going to be bumpier than I thought. I needed to keep my eyes open and be even more open-minded. I admit I didn't always display this attitude because everyone around me knew how upsetting my situation was to me, but people today are still surprised at everything I now do despite those obstacles.

7

I WANT MY LIFE BACK

While I remained a patient at Spaulding, I heard stories from my family about the worst conditions I struggled through before Spaulding (like the emergency surgeries I was rushed into at Boston Medical Center). Little by little, more of my friends from school, skating, or dance, or neighborhood came to visit. It was great to see them but also emotionally difficult for them and for me. It was hard for some people to see how different I was. I wasn't a great conversationalist, I still had that post-injury look, and I'd get really tired. For some, it was too hard to see me after I had changed so much.

Frequently when I really was in a sad state of mind, I watched the "Get well soon" video or read the card my fourth-grade class had made for me. Whenever I watched or read these materials, it was another form of motivation for me. It kept me thinking of what I really wanted and what I had to keep dedicated about, to heal enough, move out, go home, and then back to school. I knew it would take a lot of effort, but I believed in myself.

However, as months passed and patients came and went, it seemed like a few other patients and I were the only ones left. It was all a moving target. My family traded off with who stayed with me for each night. I laughed when we were together and cried as they left. I wanted to go home, I wanted to walk again, be with my friends and family, and I wanted to go back in time and stop the accident from ever happening. Or at the very least change it so that I wasn't so limited. I went to therapy sessions for my exercises every day, went through Botox injections to loosen the tightness in my body, and worked as hard as I could. Bit by bit, I continued to improve. I graduated from the electric standing table to a smaller portable one that could be used both in physical therapy and even moved to my hospital room. I was more social as I got better. I enjoyed the hospital outings each week and the time with my nurses and therapists. Time had stood still before, but it slowly moved again.

When it was still summer, some of my physical therapy sessions were held outside on the pier of Massachusetts Eye and Ear Infirmary, to which the Spaulding Pediatric Ward was attached at the time. This was where I was first introduced to AccesSportAmerica. The director, Ross Lilley, had dedicated his life to adapted sports. His son, Josh, has cerebral palsy. Ross formed the organization to enable Josh and people with any disability to partake in various sports on the dock. Ross and the other AccesSportAmerica volunteers had no qualms about taking anyone and putting them on a windsurfer, bike, hand cycle, or rock-climbing wall. My favorite of all the sports they offered by far was windsurfing. When I heard it was offered there, I was not sure I'd be able to do it. I only knew that Dad had done it in the past and that windsurfing took a lot of balance. However, I wanted to try. Ross had hooked a stander to the board, and with this addition, I held myself up and grabbed it if I lost my balance. I always loved my time with AccesSportAmerica because it gave me a taste of athletics again, and it also opened my eyes to new sports that were possible regardless of disability. Originally, I was used to being with them only during the summer, but after I started pool therapy at the Brighton YMCA, Mom, Dad, and I discovered that they ran a workout program in the same facility that I could join.

On November 5, 2003, I finally received my discharge from Spaulding and was able to move home. When I moved home, however, I discovered the true hardships that my disability brought. For the first few months, I couldn't go out for therapy or school; I had home therapies and got tutored. When I did go back to school and outpatient therapy that January, I also realized the harsh reality that sometimes I couldn't do something with my friends at recess in school. I stayed in the classroom, but my friends, Swathi, Michelle, and Amy, usually stayed with me until I was finished. I knew they needed fun for themselves too. Academics were another story. Due to the fact that my brain was hurt so badly, I had trouble processing and remembering information. As time went on though, I gained a better memorization ability for some general things.

That March, two days after my eleventh birthday was also a truly defining moment for my life. Before I moved home, a fund had been set up for me. On that day, the Colonial Figure Skating Club that Neill, Lara, and I represented held a fundraiser for me called A Little Piece of Heaven. This was a huge ice-skating show. It took some time before I really processed that everyone was skating for me, but it was also fascinating beyond words. So many people attended the event—friends I had grown up and skated with, so many other friends, people from school, my other extended family—it was truly unbelievable. Cameron even sang the Star Spangled Banner before the show started. Neill and Lara skated their exhibition piece together, and later Lara skated her own piece. The theater on ice group I had been with before my accident skated their newest program. Scott Smith even did his exhibition piece, and another national skater, Johnny Weir, skated in it. Lara and Neill knew him, and after they told him about the event months before, he offered to skate in it as well. He did his beautiful exhibition program too. I was able to go out on the ice while everyone took their bows and hugged me. I felt like a true member of my beloved rink again. The entire production was amazing; it was so sweet to know that they were doing it for me, and I was so happy to see so many new and old faces. It was such a special night.

The year felt as if it had such quick changes. On my last day of school at Loker, I led the fifth grade through the school, and as I took the lift down the staircase, my parents clapped enthusiastically. Neill had graduated from high school that spring, so Mom handed me his graduation cap to wear. The hall was lined with classmates, teachers, parents, and staff members who all clapped and cheered as we descended the stairs. Afterward, we all gathered together outside and took pictures with our friends, teachers, the principal, and fam-ily members. Mom had invited some people who were close to our family to our home later that day. The two I remember most were Ms. Cohen and my kindergarten teacher, Mrs. Scola. It was a great way to celebrate the graduation but also how far I had come versus where the doctors said I would be.

Let's fast-forward a few months. Transitioning from elementary school to middle school was a big adjustment. I had become a full-time student at Loker with a one-on-one teaching assistant that January. When I transferred to the middle school, nobody was sure how I would manage in such a new setting—new school, bigger campus, and with the three elementary schools merged together. I've always been a strong believer that anything is possible, so, of course, my approach was, "Okay, I know it'll be hard, especially with my brain injury, but I'll try really hard, and I can do it!" The first realization the school got about my true spirit was when there was a sixth-grade trip on which we all rode bikes up to Walden Pond in Concord, Massachusetts. The school didn't think I'd be strong enough to ride all the way because I couldn't ride a bike by myself. However, Mom, Dad, and I had all foreseen the school's resistance approaching. When it came time for the bike trip, Dad rented a tandem bicycle, and we did it together. Everyone got to the pond, and we spent a few hours there, seeing Henry David Thoreau's house, Emerson's home, and studying more of the surroundings. The school had prepared a bus to take me back, which I instantly rejected. I felt great, enjoyed the trip down, and was ready for another. Enthusiastically, I mounted the bike again with Dad's help, and we completed the expedition back with the rest of my classmates.

During that year, and the next years following, I became increasingly involved in physical activities. Mom, Dad, and I learned that AccesSportAmerica led a soccer clinic in Concord once a week. The soccer clinic was an important contribution to my physical improvement and athleticism. AccesSportAmerica got a full nod in helping my physical abilities develop. It was a win-win situation.

There I made more friendships with other trainers and volunteers. The first day at the clinic, I met Duncan, a volunteer who helped me run on the floor during drills and games; he was also Ross's nephew. I quickly became best friends with three of the volunteers,

Miles, Duncan, and Hannah, who was the daughter of Ross whom I mentioned earlier. At most sessions, Miles and Duncan were the ones who were asked to help me work with the exercises we all did in the beginning of the sessions. The next year, Duncan had graduated from high school and was in college, but his little brother, Connor, got involved in the soccer clinic too. He and Miles were usually the ones helping me, and, of course, Connor and I quickly became close friends too. We were also the same age, which was nice since all the other athletes were older than me. All our friendships grew the more time we spent together. We laughed, joked, and encouraged each other. I had fun, and got stronger!

I also connected with Bridget Devine. She helped me at soccer with a lot of the drills, and she later became a personal care assistant for me. She took me to many of my therapy appointments, picked me up from school when I was at a play rehearsal, and be around when I was home if my mom had to work. Sometimes, Bridget and I shopped, got ice cream from Dairy Queen, and I started asking her to work me out at home. We saw each other at soccer all the time, and she was working with AccesSportAmerica from the beginning, so she really knew what I could do and how to work with me. Mom had yoga teachers at her studio, so we have yoga and Pilates mats at home. This way Bridget could have me lie down on one of the mats, and we did all the exercises Ross has the athletes do at the beginning of the soccer sessions. Bridget and I always had so much fun together, and we shared a similar sense of humor. Whenever we were driving in the car together, there was always something to laugh about. She was also the trainer who helped me my first two years at Florida Camp. The second year I participated in the camp, I was paired with her and another girl named Erica Skinner. All three of us had a blast together and always made each other laugh. We sang songs, joked with each other, and had so much fun.

One day, the three of us kept apologizing to each other, and Erica finally said, "Okay, we're saying I'm sorry too much. We're not going to say sorry anymore, we're just going to say deal with it."

It was hard to remember, but every time one of us said sorry, one of us said, "Deal with it!" Bridget even would say, "I can deal with it." That was the only reminder I needed. The three of us all had a great week together.

The following February, I also joined AccesSportAmerica's High Challenge Sports Camp, which was held in Florida during February vacation. People with all sorts of disabilities competed in various sports, such as outrigger canoe racing, tennis, running, and windsurfing. Since it was my first year at the camp, I was a little uncomfortable being away from home, but that quickly changed.

Back at school, as I entered middle and then high school, the work became more challenging, as did the emotional aspect. Days were more demanding. My stress level heightened because the work was so much more difficult. Furthermore, I auditioned for plays in middle school and was later told that the high school theater wouldn't accommodate me. Days passed in which I saw friends who ran around the school grounds together or played sports. Oh, how I wished I could have joined. I remember crying during the night and saying I just wanted my life back. Nonetheless, I knew that my learning to negotiate middle school was another indicator of my progress. The three schools altogether made the entire middle school huge, even larger than the high school. I can't remember the number of times I got lost in both middle and high schools trying to find my next classes. I made so many new friends simply by asking where a specific room was. I was probably known as "the girl who's trying to figure everything out," which I was and had no shame in that. True, it was annoying and frustrating, but I also thought it was funny, especially when I asked about one room and it happened to be literally right in front of me or it was completely in the direction opposite to the way I was heading. In life, you really need to be able to laugh at yourself on occasion.

Some special friendships with teachers even started. I still loved singing, and I built a really strong friendship with the music teacher, Stephen Murray. At first, I wasn't sure how he'd feel about having a student in a wheelchair as a member of his chorus, but I still wanted to see how I'd fit in. He was a very fun teacher, loved joking with his students, and had some of his own humorous exercises. In chorus rehearsals, he made up really funny exercises, some being tongue twisters he had us sing constantly, like "You know you need unique New York," "Irish Wrist Watch," and "Red Leather Yellow Leather." Those were just a few of many different exercises. It took a lot of practice outside of school before I could sing them correctly. Usually my tongue was sore from forming the words. They also made me laugh so much! I was in speech for one of my therapies at Spaulding Outpatient and in school, and I do believe these exercises helped my speech improve. Thanks, Mr. Murray!

That's not just how he helped me though. In seventh and eighth grades, I was also in the select chorus he directed. During the year, we did a concert at the three elementary schools, and everyone went to McDonald's for lunch. For this, Mr. Murray had to learn how to get me on and off the bus. He met with the school physical therapist and I at one of my sessions and practiced walking me to the bus, up the stairs, into one of the seats, and back out. So not only was he a fun teacher, but he wasn't nervous about helping me physically. He was a teacher I had one of my strongest friendships with. Even today, we randomly run into each other at Barnes & Noble. We'd see each other and start laughing because it was happening so much. One year, his wife even invited me to a surprise birthday party she was throwing him. I couldn't go because I would be at Sports Camp the day of it, but the fact that she invited me really made a statement of me being a special former student of his.

Singing has always been an important part of my life. In addition to elementary and middle school, I always was part of chorale in high school. In fact, when I was a senior, there was a special trip for all the musical classes to New York City. This trip included chorale, concert choir, and the a capella groups. Here we sang at the sight where most victims from the 9/11 attack had been first recovering. We sang "The Irish Blessing," and it was so special to be in such an important place. I could feel the energy; it was like some of the spirits were there and were watching us perform. Some of the most memorable things to me were when we went to the show *How to Succeed in Business* and went to the Apollo Theater. Some members even got the opportunity to get on the stage and sing; I was one of them. I sang the first verse and refrain of "My Heart Will Go On" by Celine Dion, and everybody absolutely loved it. Also on our last night, we went to Top of the Rock at Rockefeller Center. On the top level, the view almost made me cry because it was so beautiful. It was the perfect ending to an incredible trip. If singing hadn't been such a big impact on my life, I wouldn't have had such amazing vocal experiences like these.

I have always been easy to make laugh. After all, it was how I woke up from my coma. Speaking of laughter, when I was a freshman in high school, I was in a peer-tutoring class where one of the seniors made me laugh by simply pointing at me. I thought that would make a fun addition to this book, but maybe you had to have been there. I also joined an adaptive theater group called Access to Theater, which met every Saturday. These were days spent with people who either had disabilities or simply were there to help. Each session ran for six weeks. There was an acting component as well as dance, music, and visual arts activities. The group loved how easy it was to get me to laugh. Access to Theater was a great program that got people with disabilities through difficulties so that we got a taste of what professional theater was like. When I was a junior in high school, Forrest, one of my Access to Theater friends, even was my date to prom during my junior year of high school. We were just friends, but we were intermittently the center of attention at the prom. Forrest was at the time highly influenced by Michael Jackson. He had started listening to him when he was young, and by the time I met him, he knew all his songs by heart, sounded just like Michael, and knew all his dance moves. He even taught me how to moonwalk before we went to prom. We had the time of our lives. It was one of my most memorable nights.

That night and the night of my benefit back in 2004 were eye-openers to me, not so much as a realization but as a feeling of nostalgia that made me miss everything in my life before getting hurt. As time went on, and I did more things physically, I remembered the feeling of it. I wanted my life back, and as time went on, it felt as if I was slowly retrieving parts of it.

8

I CAN DO IT

In a special education program, a planning class for students with specific needs was added to a regular school day. In middle school, the subject was organizational skills. This class helped us create ways to organize how we kept everything together so that we weren't lost trying to find things that were jumbled up in mounds of papers. We also got extra help in the Resource Room. Every time any of us had a test to take, we left the classroom and entered the Resource Room where we were in a quiet location so that we wouldn't disturb any of the other students and they wouldn't disturb us. If we needed a little more time to complete our tests, we did so in this setting. As most students would understand, we always experienced an immense feeling of relief as we finished and left the room. After my accident, most of the faculty members were hesitant about my ability to handle schoolwork; although it took a lot of effort and looking past what others told me, I surpassed their expectations and moved from elementary, to middle, and then high school.

Transitioning from elementary to middle school and then high school were huge changes—new schools, new environments, and a lot of new people. It was a big school, even larger than the middle school, more work, and more changes to get used to. We had to travel to different sections of the school for our various classes. However a teaching assistant did accompany me to help me with the work and also with knowing where to go. The school also scheduled substantial trips throughout the year as part of our specific focus on a person we were studying that year. In sixth grade, as I said earlier, we learned about Henry David Thoreau and went on a bike trip to Walden Pond. In seventh grade, we studied Rachel Louise Carson and took a three-day trip to Cape Cod, and in eighth grade, we studied Dr. Martin Luther King Jr. and did a four-day trip to Washington, DC. A teaching assistant accompanied me on these trips as well as in my classes, but being in so many different places for school still took a lot of focus.

High school brought forth a whole new era in my development. There I really needed to start fending for myself more and going the extra mile to complete the work. In my sophomore year, I also started participating in the school plays. That required additional time to focus and learn lines, dances, songs, and staging. Because of that, there was more of a time crunch to get the rest of my schoolwork done. It was hard, but if I judged time correctly, I could get work done when my scenes weren't rehearsing.

Since I needed the extra help, I built strong relationships with my teachers. Apart from the Resource Room, LRT (learning resource tutoring), the students made appointments to meet with the teachers during free periods. This was helpful to the students as well as the teachers because students got the help they needed and the teachers understood what about the assignment, test, quiz, or paper confused the student. This mechanism provided a way for the teachers to get to know each of the students better and was very helpful in showing how we really learned and whether we should take a different approach. It was a great one-on-one opportunity for both the teachers and the student.

When it came time for students to apply to college, my potential schools constituted a very short list. The four schools I applied to were Dean College, Curry College, Mass Bay Community College, and Mitchell College; these schools had the needed supports, especially for a first-time student. My guidance counselor at the high school told my parents she didn't think I could get into Curry. That sounded familiar. I applied and got in. I had previously visited Mitchell College where I met with one of the admissions officers of a partnering school, who essentially gave me a mini interview.

He said he was impressed with my outlook and determination because he asked, "How can we make sure your needs will be accessible?"

I said, "If I'm still in a wheelchair, I'll need to make sure I can navigate the campus and access the resources."

He liked that I worded it this way because I said "if," meaning that I had a major goal and that I believed in this major goal even though it would be hard.

I was accepted by three of them. The school that didn't accept me was Mitchell College; they did not only because my high school changed my transcript so that it appeared as if all my work was different from that of the other students even when it wasn't. I really liked that school, so I was a little heartbroken when in a meeting with the admissions officer I had met before, he revealed that information. After that, however, things looked up and improved. I was admitted to the other schools, and two of them gave me scholarships—not full ones but enough to help. After months in which pros and cons were weighed, I decided that Dean College was the best fit. It offered a great campus, the administration believed I would do well, and everyone was extremely friendly and inviting.

Choosing among those three schools was still a very difficult decision, but it felt so good to accomplish yet another thing that my parents had been told I wouldn't be able to do.

When my parents met with my special education teacher, guidance counselor, and school physical therapist, they were told again and again that I was unable to complete work by myself, that my grades on tests were very low, that I never sequenced an essay correctly on my own, I couldn't graduate in four years, wouldn't be able to pass MCAs or the other exams in school, and (without using the specific words) I couldn't get into college. I attended some of these meetings in my senior year but hadn't in the years before. Whenever I asked my parents what went on and they told me, frustration just burned throughout my entire body. Dismissal can be very upsetting, even if it seems unimportant to others. Nevertheless, I turned to my original strategy: took what they said and turned it into motivation, allowing myself to push further than my potential appeared to the human eye. After my final grades were in, it was clear that the next year I would join my fellow classmates at graduation.

Graduation brought its own difficulties, however. The entire senior year, my school physical therapist, and I had planned for me to use my cane for the walk across the stage while two of my friends, Seth and Caleb, spotted me. We did great at the first graduation rehearsal, but for the next, I wore a device that stimulated my leg with a thirty-second vibration and helped my foot come up higher. I had not quite gotten used to it though, so it threw my balance off. Long story short, the school PT didn't want me to walk by myself; Caleb had to hold my elbow. I was not a happy camper, especially since we had planned on my doing it independently with Caleb and Seth there just to spot me. I came home, told my parents, and cried angry tears for an hour. That was far from the last emotional outburst I had about my situation, but it was always followed up by a voice in my head that told me, "It's okay, but don't let it overtake you." I listened and then moved on. I then told myself, *Marina, crying isn't going to change anything, only you can.*

This may have been a new issue, but it wasn't going down without a fight. Long story short, my parents got involved, and there were a lot of e-mails. Thankfully, the physical therapist agreed I could walk independently if Caleb still spotted me, but she needed to be behind me as well instead of having Seth. On graduation day, when my name was called, the three of us made our way across the stage, but I was walking with my cane completely independently, with Caleb and the physical therapist behind me. I was too focused to look around, but later my parents said I got a standing ovation, first from all the seniors and then everyone else who came to the ceremony. Jolts of joy and excitement swept the entire field, encompassing all the graduates, parents, teachers, friends, and anyone who attended. After the ceremony ended, the first two people who ran up to give me huge hugs were Caleb's brothers, Jonah and Isaac, also two of my best friends. It was a day of truth, determination, commitment, belief, joy, and completion that I will never forget.

Outside of school, I cleared a number of major hurdles. One summer, my parents and I took a trip to Greece. It was my first time there, and I knew it was going to be different from what we usually did. It wasn't easy, but I loved it. One day, Mom wanted to show me the Acropolis, which we had a great view of from a hotel. The day we went to it was so hot. I had to keep sitting down and taking sips of water because I was so out of breath. Despite the heat and the distance, I knew I had to keep going. I was fighting an internal conflict with myself, one side saying stop and the other was saying "Keep going, you can do it!" I kept walking and made it all the way up with Dad. If I hadn't had the belief in my heart, I wouldn't have accomplished the goal of seeing this immensely significant site.

9

LONG AND HARD

Summers were really the time when my strength grew the most. Because I wasn't in school, I had time to focus more on my body. I still went to therapy appointments. Mom frequently took me to the ballet studio where I walked along the bar, and when we went up to Maine, I almost never used my wheelchair unless we were out to dinner or going around town. I even brought my quad cane up every year and regularly practiced walking by myself on the beach. Dad was usually behind me in case I fell. Mom filmed it most of the time so that later I could look at the video and visualize what I needed to change, whether it is my foot placement, the cane tipping, or if I needed to straighten up. Now I know some people might have assumed that I was only exercising over the summer, but for three summers, I attended a theater camp at the high school, another day camp in Cochituate, and then there was always Maine. There, we swam, rode bikes, went to the beach, and flat-out enjoyed not having a schedule that needed to be followed. It was such a special place.

Week by week, month by month, year by year dragged by, and I was still not where I wanted to be mobility-wise. Still I pushed past the negative messages my brain sent me and kept my eyes on the prize. I saw myself running again. Mom told me she kept having dreams about that as did the adapted gym teacher at Loker, John Passarini. Before my accident, I used to volunteer at his adapted classes to assist students who had disabilities. He was always over-joyed when he saw me. After I left the hospital and went back to school, he even talked to my parents and me about a half-marathon held every year in memory of a girl who had died from complications of dwarfism years ago. I remembered that half-marathon and after a few months decided to set completing it as a goal. For the first two years, I did the Purple Shoes Challenge, which was a portion conducted inside the gym. It was a good way to start, especially so as to work up to longer distances. The next year, I did the 5k. I rode the first two miles on my bike and walked for the final mile. I rode and walked, using my walker, with Dad. Mom followed us in her car. Lara joined behind us, and Julia Schecter, our friend from skating, walked with Lara. Doing the 5k for the first time provided me my greatest sense of accomplishment so far. It took just under two hours, but I did it! It felt so incredible to be back as a member of a group with Mr. Passarini again after I had volunteered in his classes at school. Maybe I wasn't exactly where I wanted to be, but each day, I felt myself getting stronger and closer to the light that burned in the distance.

I felt that everyone I knew was always there for me. At school, my teachers knew how hard I worked, my therapists saw my drive in sessions, my family saw all the dedication and motivation in my eyes, and my friends saw how I took in everything and did my best with problems that needed to be solved. The one exception was, as I said earlier, that my high school administration didn't think I could successfully go to college and changed my transcript in such a way that one of the schools to which I applied did not accept me. Nevertheless, I was accepted into the three other colleges. I've said this all along: "Even though someone thought you couldn't achieve a goal, don't give up right away. These things might take more time than you want, but if you hang on, you can reach the top of the mountain." The progression is always hard and always takes a lot of effort, but from my perspective, little by little, the outcome will be worth the struggles.

10

IS THIS WORTH IT?

Throughout this book, I've told you that I have had a strong and confident attitude regarding my disability, but even I have my difficult days. As I watched people leaving Spaulding before me, friends I skated with moving up to higher levels, and people in my grade at school moving into harder classes, I wondered when my time would be. I tried not to let my tribulations overtake me. I tried to stay as positive as possible by keeping busy with friends, focusing in therapy, and along the way believing that I just needed to wait a little longer.

Even at home, there were some days when I just looked out my window to keep focused on something other than the continuing frustration about my disability and the things I couldn't do. I simply didn't have the same life I had before my accident, and it annoyed me that no matter how hard I tried, I still had not gotten to the level I wanted to obtain. Still I worked as hard as I could in therapies and kept up my inner strength. A voice and energy inside told me that if I hung in, I was in for a tremendous surprise. Whenever I was in a dark place, I heard that voice and always kept going. Maybe things weren't quite the way they used to be, I told myself, but I was the one who needed to figure out how far I could get. Each hurdle I managed to face with courage was just a test. Thankfully, as I listened to that voice, I pressed through the annoyance and pain that came with my disability and used it to my own advantage—and eventually not only my own advantage but that of many others as well.

My family and I still traveled, often to places where Neill and Lara were skating in ice shows after they transitioned from competitors to professionals, and sometimes we encountered an unfamiliar state or country that had less-than-perfect forms of accessibility. My experience in such places helped in two ways because we saw what needed to be improved, and people there actually saw what caused someone with disabilities to struggle. Two of the most inaccessible places were Holland and Germany. After figuring out how to get me through an obstacle, residents of the country were able to see the struggle, and hopefully they knew how to fix an obstacle so that other disabled people could get through easily. Traveling was beneficial for both knowing what needed to be improved for me and others in a similar situation.

A funny story from Holland occurred on our first day there. My parents and I wandered outside and walked around to see the surroundings. As we went along, we saw a section of the road with yellow paint halfway down each lane. When Mom and I first saw that, we both thought they had made a wheelchair path on the road. Wrong. Shortly after we began our walk, out of nowhere someone on a bicycle zoomed past us. Abruptly, we sped to the side of the road. After that bicyclist passed, we turned back outward to the street. No sooner did we do so that, another bicyclist came racing passed us. Again, my parents rushed over to the side with me. This happened a few more times, and we all thought people just hadn't paid attention. We then came across a sign on the road; it clearly said "Bicycle Lane." The three of us looked at one another and burst out into laughter. That explained why we almost got run over.

Nighttime in Amsterdam was another story. Our hotel was right by a nightclub called Royalty. I looked longingly at it whenever we passed it as we returned to our hotel. I really wanted to go, but it was a twenty-one and up nightclub, and I was fifteen at the time. Well, after a few days when the bouncers had noticed the look on my face as we passed, one night they told my parents I could go in. Long story short, it was such a fun club, and I danced a lot. That night, I met so many people who danced with me. One was even a physiotherapist who got me out of my wheelchair when we danced and carried me to different sections of the room. However, there was one thing I hadn't realized. He was on a pub crawl, and he tried to leave for another bar with me. Dad thankfully stopped him. After that night, my parents and I went to the club for a total of three nights, but unfortunately, I never saw my friend again in Amsterdam at night, and this memory in particular are definitely something I'll never forget.

Throughout Amsterdam, my family and I visited many different sites. We saw Castle De Harr, a palace, and various museums. The skating show Neill and Lara were in was very entertaining. It was a live-band concert complete with a full orchestra and a stage made of ice right above them. Amsterdam was a completely diverse scene from where Neill and Lara competed before they turned professional. After all, show life is a very different scene from competition. Also we all really needed to get used to the time zone difference. My parents and I took naps in the middle of the day so we made it through the nights. I was so jet-lagged when we came home. I went back to school with so many stories of an amazing trip that it made its challenges worth it.

After we were home for a few days, life was routine again. School went on, and I watched my friends as they ran off at times. I worked as hard as I could in therapies, but I still did not gain the amount of strength and balance I wanted. Still, I told myself, I had to wait a little longer, but I would walk again. I continued with appointments. I visited Spaulding on occasion and was told about other patients who were in wheelchairs while I was there who had walked back in when they visited. Envy and anger bubbled up inside of me, but I never showed it. Now that I think about it, maybe I did. I tried to keep it all to myself. I was working so hard; everyone knew how much I wanted my independence back. I was a respectful patient while in Spaulding; why hadn't it paid off yet? Why had it seemed like I gave so much effort but got nothing back in return? I had been told so many times that I would not be in a wheelchair that much longer. Why had I sometimes been told that it would happen in a shorter time frame? Why not now?

Although I knew I was an example people looked up to because of my spirit and "never give up" attitude, I started to wonder if everything I did in therapy exercises truly did its job or whether I set myself up to climb to a mountain's summit that could not be reached. However, I relegated that thought to the back of my mind and tried not to let it cloud my optimism because I knew if I kept a good state of positivity, it would walk with me down this path. I pushed past that odious phrase "accidents will happen" because I thought that saying only allowed people to think whatever happened to themselves or others was not a big deal. I had a vision of being freed, and I never wanted to let that slip my mind, whether other people believed in me or not. It all went back to what I said earlier in this chapter—sometimes only you can determine an unresolved scenario.

Maybe that is the main lesson about life.

Life is great and full of new experiences, but the bumps along the way are tests we face. Those tests show how much we can take before reaching a breaking point and perhaps find what motivates us. Sometimes when we ask the question "Is this worth it?" we discover the true meanings of life and the sense of belongingness and awareness we need to accept. There were times when I began down a wrong path that only reached negative outlooks and endings. When this happened, I heard a voice in my head again that said I needed to keep believing even though things were not good for me right then and there. Again and again, I heard the words, "Is this worth it? You've worked so hard and come such a long way with your progress. Are you really going to let a little frustration get the better of you? If you do, you'll never get the outcome you want and set out for from the moment you woke up from your coma." Is this worth it? That is the real question life asks us.

11

GIVING UP

If I had considered giving up, it never lasted. I knew that wasn't in the cards I was dealt. In fact, as time went on, more possibilities emerged. For the crew team I was on, I won my first CRASHBS (Charles River Association of Sculling Has-Beens), a world indoor rowing sprint competition. I was also on a list for a service dog for six years because we learned that it would help me live more independently. I needed a hypoallergenic dog because Mom and Lara are so allergic to golden retrievers; the organization was not able to find the right kind of dog for me, so Mom talked to a woman at our church who told us about APAW, an organization based in Spencer, Massachusetts. They work only with poodles, which was exactly what I needed. I met a poodle named Twinkle in October. Service dogs undergo a whole training routine, so I worked with Twinkle from October through May. Interestingly, she and I graduated from the organization just after I had graduated from Dean. I graduated as a cum laude student too. My high school said I couldn't do it; well, I did.

Twinkle was such a good help to me. Whenever I dropped or could not reach something, I would have Twinkle run over and retrieve it for me or get what I needed. When she was in the right mood, Twinkle always became very playful and energetic. If she was bored, she came over to me and jumped around and gave me this playful look. Sometimes she gave a short and playful bark. If she could talk, I understood her bark to say, "Marina! I'm bored and you're so much fun! Play with me!" Sometimes she even nipped at the air. Mom and I figured out that when she did this, it was the way she "talked." Most of the times she did this, it was cute. Occasionally, though, it annoyed us, especially if we were busy with something else.

Twinkle was always such a great companion to me. She never left my side even if her attention was on something other than me. Even when I wrote, she was underneath the table. She was another reason I never gave up. I knew that everything Twinkle could do for me only added to all I wanted ability-wise in my life. Unfortunately, she got kicked out of my college (she growled and barked sometime), and then APAW decided she wasn't the right match for me and took her back after we had trained so much together and she had been given to me. Her loss was devastating to me. That was another situation where emotional strength had to kick in.

I knew there was potential in my future to regain everything I wanted back, but I couldn't do it alone. For years I had wondered if I would ever meet someone who knew what I had gone through. In one simple week, that changed. One day, Mom's cell phone rang while she was driving us to an appointment, so I answered it for her. The caller was Peter Halby, director of a number of entities focused on supporting people with disabilities; he had called to invite me to a camp held in Vermont held by the Love Your Brain foundation that was specifically for traumatic brain injury survivors. In 2010, Kevin Pearce was a favorite snowboarder who had trained for the Winter Olympics that next year. He had mastered an extremely hard trick called the double cork in which he jumped very high and did two sideways flips in the air. This time, however, he crashed face first into the snow. He was unconscious and in a heavy coma at a hospital where he almost died. I'm not belittling what he went through, but my journey was similar. My family experienced the same pain his family struggled through, wondering if he would survive his coma. They, too, feared losing the youngest son, a little brother—and in his case, a true icon of the snowboard Hall of Fame. Finally, however, he awakened, did months of therapy, and became an icon of hope for others. He later met Peter Halby and expressed to him the wish that he could form a camp for other traumatic brain injury survivors.

When he vocalized this desire, Pete then said, "Well, actually we have land in Vermont and we've got a camp."

You can guess what happened next. Kevin and his brother, Adam Pearce, began the Brainfarmers Retreat as a program of their Love Your Brain Foundation to be held in the spring. This gave survivors the opportunity to share stories, support each other, understand how the outcome changed each person, and learn further how a future can be obtained if approached the right way. For me it was an amazing week; I hadn't known anybody who had an injury like mine. My friends, Mark Young and Rey Vasquez, whom I had met at Florida High Challenge Sports Camp, was there as well. I hadn't known before that a stroke, which they had both suffered, technically was considered a traumatic brain injury. Everyone who attended the camp had a traumatic brain injury; some had family members with them for support, but I was the only one in a wheelchair. Lara had gone home with my parents after they dropped me off. However, they watched *The Crash Reel*, a movie about Kevin's journey, that night, which brought all the painful memories back to Lara. This evoked her realization that she wanted to come back and be with me. When Lara came back, she helped my one-on-one trainer, Julie Potter, to walk me around since I did not like using my chair most of the time.

The first day of camp, I entered the main room with an open mind, not sure how we'd all be together. The days consisted of a lot of support groups, swimming, yoga, and meditation every morning. After yoga, we all sat in a circle, and people talked about anything on their minds or even coping strategies if we were upset. I met a young man named Grant. He was my age, and we became close friends. Anytime I needed help, he was usually the first to run over and push my chair or help Julie support me while we walked. Whenever I got out of my chair, he'd help me stand up and help me balance while I walked. I remember Adam specifically coming up to me and commenting that whenever I had something to say to the entire camp, he could feel an energy coming from everybody there as they really listened to me. I had never realized how powerful things I had to say were. Being with everyone from the Brainfarmers always felt so empowering because we could all be together and understand what each of us went through. We loved hanging out together. It was always great to be surrounded by these friends during the retreat.

Lara and I had also formed a strong friendship with a young man named Connor Derraugh. He always walked around and chatted with us when we hung out. He was a fun person, and I felt as if we connected as well. Connor's brother, Tyler, was there too. He was a speed skater, so he and Lara connected, especially on the skating topic. That year, I hadn't signed up for the Vermont City Marathon in time for the retreat, but there was a walk the day before, open to for any of us to participate in. However, after the marathon, somebody was at the bus before I got on. She had done the marathon and received a medal. When I got up to her, she took the medal from around her neck and put it on me, saying, "You deserve this more than me." I was shocked and so honored.

The following year, I did sign up for the marathon, and I rode a hand cycle for the 5k portion of it. The next year, my third with Love Your Brain, I used the hand cycle for a 10k. I don't remember how long either of these took me before I officially finished, but that didn't matter. As we got off the bus back at Zeno, my friend, Maggie, who was my one on one helper that week, walked me down the row of seats. Adam was standing at the top of the steps looking at me with a big smile, and when I got up to him, he took his medal from around his neck, put it around me, and said, "You deserve this." I had conquered more obstacles that stood in my way because I never gave up.

One summer at the dock in Boston where the Adaptive Sports summer program was held, I met a man named Joe who later started doing the Love Your Brain retreats. He was really into windsurfing and the other sports as well. We and our respective parents became really good friends too; he and his family lived up in Maine, so we all got to see each other in Goose Rocks sometimes. He and I also went to gait training as part of our physical therapy, and he did the Sports Camp in Florida as well.

At the first Love Your Brain retreat, I met a girl named Sage who was also a first-time attendee, and we became fast friends. She did all the Brainfarmers retreats too. One day during the first retreat, Lara and I met her mom who had on a T-shirt that said, "I love my TBI survivor." She told us she made them regularly, so Lara and I ordered some. My shirt has the title "Traumatic Brain Injury Survivor" on it. It is one of my favorite shirts because I feel that it represents my strength as it does for the other survivors. Whenever I've worn it, I've always felt a strong power because it gives me so much more confidence.

The thing that has always been a positive are all the people from Zeno Mountain Farm. Although there are various places where their camps and retreats are held, the main base of Zeno is in Lincoln, Vermont. During the summer, they run a very involved camp for the full month of July. Even though some people are invited for the month, others for two weeks week, some for only one week. I've been invited for the last two weeks every year since I graduated from high school. The second two weeks of the camp focus on producing a play in which everyone is fully included. What's so great about staying there is that after spending so much time together, you really feel like everybody there is your family and Zeno is a home. That's what it feels like when you first arrive and go through the doors of the Main House; you have come home. There's so much adrenaline about seeing old friends, meeting new people, doing various activities during the day, and events in the evenings. Of course, the main focus is on the production of the play, especially when we know there is a short time frame to memorize lines, songs, create scenes, and learn anything else that is included in the involvement. Luckily, when friends become family, everything seems easier.

Sometimes, people may think that starring in movies or plays is only for people who are able-bodied. That stereotype couldn't be more wrong. Each year, Zeno ran both a film camp in California, and the summer play at Zeno in Vermont. Sometimes in life, people with disabilities are judged because of their differences. Once people arrive at Zeno, all that frustration and judgment deteriorates as we interact with everybody and all have equal opportunities. We have to commit to the play, but we also take opportunities to go on outings as well. For instance, one day we all took a bus to Six Flags, and occasionally, we went to outdoor concerts. Some days we even went horseback riding. Everyone was amazed when I got back on a horse. It was such a powerful experience even though it wasn't my first time back up on a horse since my accident. During camp, there is always something to do, and we leave with memories that last forever.

People are nervous when they walk into a new circumstance for their first time, not knowing how they will fit in with so many new people. Once they go through the doors at Zeno, however, they are welcomed with open arms and have that tingling of excitement when people come up to meet them. Unlike Love Your Brain retreats where everyone but the aids and people running it have a traumatic brain injury, everyone who attends the Zeno camps has some type of disability, and each attendee is paired up with an aid or two one-on-one. Some of these disabilities can consist of cerebral palsy to down syndrome to Williams Syndrome. As soon as they are welcomed, they are engulfed with a flurry of people introducing themselves, conversations, and stories. This is far from your typical summer camp. Instead of staying in cabins, campers lived and those who work for Zeno stay in adapted tree houses. Each has its own way for people to get in. In the tree houses, we can literally see the trunk of the tree growing through with the house built around it. Inside each house there are bunk beds, but not just what you would expect. The posts of each one are made of tree branches, and we can even hang jackets and towels off them. The tree houses really feel like a real home rather than a cabin at camp. At Zeno, whenever somebody has emotional struggles, we can be sure that there is always somebody there to support and help talk us through it. That's another thing that is so special about coming to Zeno Mountain Farm. Each person has at least one person who will always be there for them. This is all what makes Zeno Mountain Farm such a special and sacred place.

Back in 2003, when I first moved home from the hospital, I saw so many negatives in my disability, but now ever since my hard work, I've felt so much stronger. Whenever I thought about my disability, the conclusion I came up with was that it was only a pain at first, some days literally, but my hard work on account of it was worth it so much more in the end.

Similarly, whenever I consider the challenges I have faced, it gets me to really think about what it takes to be confident and to continue to believe in yourself. Maybe in our lives, we are faced with ever more challenging situations to see how much we can handle. That might not match some challenges people undergo, but it is an optimistic and considerate way of thinking. We'll never know the answer to such questions, but they should make you think. My mantra is treat the challenges you meet as your enemies, and they will not be as hard.

12

SUPPORT

I associate support with finding buried treasure. You keep searching for it and then when it's found, you cherish it because you were so committed to it. Personally, I love going around and helping people with anything that's hard for them, but what's nice is when they help me as well. I am only one person, and, of course, I want to solve everybody's problems, but there are many times when I need the same thing. It is then that I am so thankful to know somebody is there to sustain me. As I think through the struggles that have come alongside my expeditions, I realize that I have never been without someone behind me to help me to finish them. Without that support from my friends, doctors, family, therapists, professors, and countless others, I don't know where I would be now.

Every time I took my tests in the learning center, someone read the questions for me. It was then that my parents and I realized I did better when I heard the information instead of just reading it. The readers for my tests were usually my notetakers. I had the same three of them for both semesters those two years. One was a man named Rob who was a resident director of one of the dorms. He took notes in two of my classes, and outside of class, we got to be really good friends. There were even some days when we were both in the dining hall (where I helped wipe down tables after dinner when I didn't need to get a lot of work done) at the same time, and we sat and ate together. I felt that he was more a friend to me than my notetaker. Even outside the classes he took notes for, we talked and laughed together. My other notetakers were the wife of the Dean of Students (who also became a good friend) and for math only, a member of the Math Department. These people always made me feel welcomed, and not that I should be separated because of my learning challenges.

Things got a little hard, however, especially when it came to academics at Dean College. When I first moved into Dean as a full-time student, the workload was heavier and harder than I was used to. Luckily, because of the meetings and orientation tours I had attended in the beginning of the semester, I had an idea of the campus layout and how to approach professors. As the year went on, I learned the right strategies over how to get extra help, especially whenever I had a long-term assignment. My routine tended to be going to the writing center, doing my schoolwork, seeing tutors before tests, and have writing tutors edit paper drafts the other students and I had done. I became friendly with one of the professional writing tutors and saw him constantly whenever I had a draft of a paper. The writing center wasn't the only place where students got extra help though; professors were always available outside of class during their office hours at specific times as well. They each had specific times at which any student could meet with them, whether they simply wanted to have a meeting, needed extra help on a topic, or, like me, had to get a green sheet signed for the extra accommodations for tests.

In my first years at Dean, the learning center wanted them a week in advance of the tests. Sometimes, I had a reminder from my parents or I wrote on a sticky note that I needed to get a sheet, and eventually I kept extra sheets in my dorm room. When I handed them in early, it was a huge weight off my shoulders. Sometimes, I got really stressed out about my forgetfulness, but mistakes happen.

The second semester of that year, I even had the dean of students as my professor for sociology. He was very supportive and helpful with the work his students did, even when I saw him about papers and tests. I thought that he would have been too busy to give extra time to his students. I also consulted an academic coach who helped me to sort out my assignments and keep myself organized, saw my advisor or another professor if I felt overwhelmed at any point, kept in touch with my family, and made a habit of working in the writing center. When Neill had time at home between skating contracts, he came to Dean and tutored me. No matter how hard a subject was, little by little I improved. Second semester was even more difficult, but with hard work and dedication, I made it through.

In my second year at Dean, I took abnormal psychology because I thought it sounded interesting and would not be too challenging. Boy, was I wrong. Most of the semester I was failing it, but I got a ton of help from tutors in the writing center a lot, and at the end of the semester, I finished with a C. It was a huge improvement from where I was. That same year, more things started looking up. After months of training sessions in the evening meetings at school, I was inducted into the National Society of Leadership and Success. During the ceremony, all the inductees and I sat clapping for everyone as we anxiously awaited our names being called. When my name was called, I drove my chair to one end of the stage, and then two members who were part of the faculty assisted me out of my chair and helped me as I walked across the stage. Everyone who sat in the audience screamed and clapped for me as I walked. The resident director of my dorm and the man who was the chapter leader at Dean for the National Society of Leadership and Success both stood at the far end of the podium to give me the Society certificate, and then they both separately pulled me into their arms and hugged me. After the ceremony had ended, some of my friends who were watching said I made them cry tears of joy. It was an amazing experience and a nod to my capabilities.

I really don't know where I'd be right now without all this strength behind me. My doctors at Boston Medical Center even said that one reason I recovered so well was because my family never left my side. True, they had their own lives to take care of, but someone was always with me while I recovered from my accident. Back in Spaulding, if my parents had to go away, it was one of my aunt's or Marina Flessas who looked after me. My aunt Cornelia, a professor at Rhode Island School of Design, frequently brought etching plates for me to scratch a drawing on, then she made a print by spreading ink across the plate, laying a piece of paper down, and running it through a press. To this day, I still have those prints. After I moved home from rehab, she had me sign one that we did when I was first coming out of my coma; this, of course, was an example that showed how far I had come.

The support through friendship only grew when I entered middle and high school. I started getting migraines in eighth grade, but when I entered my freshman year at Wayland High School, they got worse and more frequent. Sometimes, they were so bad I couldn't listen to anything, focus, or look anywhere comfortably. One day during my junior year at a rehearsal for the school play, I noticed my head bothering me even after I had taken Tylenol earlier that day. The minutes ticked by, and I finally couldn't sing our songs, keep my head out of my hand, or keep my eyes open because I was in so much pain. Dad came to get me after rehearsal, and I was still in the same state. I told him what was wrong, and as he pushed me out of the room, I saw a number of my closest friends watching me leave. It was clear to me they were concerned, wondering if I'd be okay.

The year I was a junior in high school, my parents and I had researched baclofen pumps. My physiatrist had seen me move my left leg a certain way, and he said I might qualify for one. This is a device that would be implanted into my abdomen and have a catheter that wrapped halfway around my back. I had become used to all my surgeries, so even before I went in, I wasn't worried. My parents and I were told I'd be at that hospital for the day and then be transferred over to rehab afterward, or so we thought. In fact, after the operation, I had to stay at the hospital for the week because I was having constant spinal headaches. They didn't want me transferred until I was ambulatory, but for days, I couldn't sit up for extended periods of time without throwing up. After a few days, I finally started crying because I wanted to go to rehab since that way I'd know I was improving. After that week, I went to Braintree Rehab for another week. There I befriended my therapists, nurses, doctors, and some of the patients.

When I first got there, we discovered something my parents and I hadn't factored into consideration at all: they couldn't stay with me. They visited me every day, but most of the time, I cried when it was time for them to leave. Being in a hospital by myself was hard at first. It was a brand-new experience for me. However, having my cell phone made it easier, so I called my friends back home, talked to my siblings, and I had a lot of visitors. Since my surgery was before the school year ended, a teacher with whom I was friendly came and tutored me. I had still been on my adapted crew team, so my coach, Cristina, and Dave, who helped with the team, came in occasionally. Dave even brought me a new game, Bannanagrams, on one of his visits. I played it all the time with Mom and Dad whenever they came.

It wasn't until then that we realized something else about me. After the pump was put in, I began to have terrible migraines. Once at a play rehearsal that fall, my head hurt so much that I finally couldn't sing any of the songs, lift my head out of my hand, or keep my eyes open because I was in so much pain. At one point when my eyes were open, out of my peripheral vision, I saw Gabe giving me a really concerned look. I turned to look at him. He mouthed "Are you okay?" and I just closed my eyes, shook my head, and put an arm out, signaling him not to worry about it. I stayed that way through the rest of rehearsal, and when Dad came to get me when rehearsal ended, I told him how much pain I was in as I fought back tears. As he pushed my wheelchair out of the room, I could see Gabe, Jonah, and my friends, Seth, Patricia, Dan, and Lizzie, all watching me leave, hoping that I'd be okay.

The purpose of the surgery just mentioned was to control the spasticity that had overtaken my body since the accident. Spasticity is what is keeping me in a wheelchair. Since my muscles are tight, my balance gets thrown off easily. Therefore, prior to the surgery, it was nearly impossible to walk or at least to walk well. The pump is designed to shoot liquid muscle relaxant to the tight, or spastic, areas in my body. However, after the surgery, when the pump took away all the spasticity that my body was used to having, it took me some weeks to adjust to the absence of spasticity; evidently, the spasticity had actually helped my balance, so I had to learn how to walk without it. Several months after the surgery, some of the spasticity returned. One of my doctors told me I was beginning to override it, so there was hope.

We all need to have regard for and faith in ourselves. Easier said than done, but I believe that in even the simplest circumstances, no matter how hard a task may seem, we must believe that there is hope and that the situation will improve. I know how difficult it is for those with challenges to read these words at first, regardless of what the scenario is, but in order to survive, we really must keep believing, put ourselves out there, and see what can be done. It is important, too, to have faith in one's own judgment. We have all been there at some point in life, questioning our choices. We should never let what someone else says mess with our minds and make us second-guess a decision. Some things work out when you least expect them to do so.

Many people say that there is a meaning for the events that take place in our lives. Well, few people actually seem able to put that philosophy into practice. The closest I've ever come to believing it was Christmas in 2015. My grandfather gave me an assortment of books, one of which was entitled *Everything Happens for a Reason* by Mira Kirshenbaum. That book so intrigued me that it would've taken me no more than a day to read if I hadn't been so busy in my daily life; while I was reading it, it sounded as if it really could have been written by a Greek philosopher. As I read each chapter, each reason described, I found myself nodding and saying to myself, "Okay, that really makes sense." The writer literally cites just about every possible reason why something bad happens to a person and delves into all the various reasons for its forthcoming. Personally, I've always believed things happen to a person to show them how strong they are. At least that's the perspective I forced myself to take when I finally understood possible reasons for what really happened to me.

Another function of support, as I think everyone can agree, is that when you have people behind you, tasks can be completed much easier. I remember that there were some days, and are some even now, when I would burst into tears and collapse in my mom's, dad's, or Lara's arms when I couldn't do what I wanted to do. I'm generally a strong, optimistic, and motivated person, but as I said in an earlier chapter, I still have my dark days. I'm only human, so it's normal, but sometimes that's hard for me to accept. At times, I just have to admit that I don't understand why it's taking me so long to get my full mobility back because I've been working for so long and so hard. When I was younger, I gave myself a harder time when that happened. Now that I've grown older, I let myself break down a little more. I used to blame myself for having my accident because I wanted to start riding; I was so desperate to find a reason for its happening.

It is nice to have people who support you so much when you need it. Once at a play rehearsal in high school, the theater teacher and director commented that people use the excuse that "it was an accident," but he said, "Accidents don't exist. The person who says something was an accident always bears some responsibility."

I knew that he wasn't directing that to me and that he meant no harm, but it really reinforced the blame I put on myself since I was ten. My friend Gabe clearly saw that I was upset, so he took me off stage and brought me into the band room to talk to me about what was wrong. When he closed the door, I burst into uncontrollable sobs. I felt guilty that he had to see me so upset, but I knew that at that moment, he wanted to be there for me. We had met the year before and became best friends. That's what made it easy to talk to him. I remember Gabe listening intently to everything I said to him; that was one of the first times I let a high school friend see how torn apart I still was over my accident. Most of the time, I generally didn't talk about it and tried not to let people see me as such a mess.

After I finished weeping and got my breath back, he comforted me, talking soothingly and reassuring me that it wasn't my fault; he gave me a hug, and we went back into the theater. I was so thankful that I had a close friend with me for support and trust. He made me feel so much better. To this day, I remember that situation as if it was yesterday, and I'll never forget it.

I didn't usually let myself get that upset, but it happened on occasion. I had been invited to dinner by our friends the Greenawalts, whose sons Caleb, Jonah, and Issac were my high schools friends. Caleb was my age, Jonah just a year younger, and Issac about three years under Caleb. That evening, another situation arose in which I completely lost control of my emotions but knew I had a friend behind me. It was just Jonah and I sitting together. Jonah and I were close friends; he even helped me transfer in and out of my wheelchair and helped me walk up the stairs when the director was holding rehearsals in the room above the theater if the set was getting painted or there was something else going on in the theater.

As we started talking that evening, a distressing memory from the time when I was in my coma tumbled out, and I burst into tears. Jonah gave me a hug, held me there, and talked to me in a soothing voice. As I put my head on his shoulder, he said, "You never told me that, Marina." He was right. I had never told anybody that story with its painful details until then because the memory of it was so personal and so hard to relive. I had decided to keep the details to myself because I knew anyone who heard them would be just as horrified and disturbed by them as I was. Once again, I was so thankful to have one of my best friends exactly the type of support that I needed.

During our senior year, Caleb and I were at the high school rehearsing for *Les Mis* together. One of my close friends, Forrest, had gone missing, and I was worried about him. Caleb was listening and taking what I had to say into consideration. He then asked about the whole story, particularly why my friend had left, if anyone knew where else to look for him, and what really made him leave. He hadn't met Forrest but knew he had taken me to my junior prom and was a special friend to me. Forrest was found a few months later, but he had really changed. It was important to me, however that Caleb wanted to support me, especially when I was concerned about my friend.

Another unforgettable instance of support occurred when Caleb and I graduated from high school. We and our friend Cato held a graduation party together. We all had a wonderful time with students from our class. After the party had come to an end, my parents and I stayed to help clean up. When we all finished, I gave something to Caleb as both a graduation present and a token to say thank you for everything we had done together that year. He was my partner in a skit we did in the winter and had become a very good friend. I had taken photos from the plays, a New York trip, and graduation, all the events we had done together and formed them into a little scrapbook for him. He loved it. Nevertheless, I burst into tears because he and

I were best friends, and I knew many people never saw their friends from high school after they graduated. He smiled, listened, then comforted me, pulled me into his arms, and said we'd see each other again. He began listing all the opportunities we'd have, like summer, college breaks, and whenever we were all home. I started laughing at how silly I was being. Now I still see them all on occasion. Caleb, Jonah, Isaac, and I were best friends and still are today. They still consider me part of their family, and I feel so thankful.

I had hoped that as I grew older, my sadness and the level at which I missed things from life before my accident would subside, but I was wrong. It wasn't that surprising as much as it was annoying. I don't like people seeing me cry, and I never want my emotions to drive me down. Once, however, I was at DSW Shoe Warehouse with Lara and Mom. Lara saw a pained expression on my face, pushed me in my chair down the aisle, sat down next to me, and let me start crying my eyes out. She wrapped me in her arms, holding me and rubbing my back.

When I had enough breath in my lungs, I said to her, "Lara, people tell me I give such good advice, and I want to help them, but sometimes it's just, what about me?"

She held me for another minute and then said, "Marina, you've been through a really hard time, and on top of that, you don't need to be a champion. I love how much you want to be there for people, and I think you do need to give a little time to that, but you always need to make sure you have time for yourself. It's a really good thing that you can feel this way and show your feelings because if you didn't, that would be really concerning."

I knew exactly what she meant. I sat up, wiped my eyes, and, when my vision was no longer clouded by tears, I saw that Mom had come up, was listening, and then gave me a hug too. Since that time, I still try to find reasons why things happen. When I fall, I try to think about what made me fall and what I can potentially do to keep standing. I try to piece together everything for what it really is.

Due to the area of my brain that I injured, I've lost a lot of physical feelings. For instance, I don't have the feeling of temperature, hunger, or when I'm full. I always say pain is the feeling I still have most of the time, but even that goes back and forth as well. This is both a problem and a convenience. Since my feeling of temperature isn't very good, I can be with my friends doing things outside for long periods of time without being too hot or too cold. When we go to Maine, sometimes I can be in the ocean for an hour. Even if my skin's bright red and my teeth are chattering, when anybody asks me if I'm cold, I always said no. Same with hunger; sometimes I can go hours without feeling that I need to eat. I sometimes forget to eat lunch at home, and that alone isn't good, especially for energy support. Luckily, someone always watches out for me in these circumstances. I have come up with strategies to figure it out though. I judge temperature by how the air feels. If it's soft and heavy, it's warm, but if it is hard and crisp, it's cold. For hunger, sometimes my stomach hurts, and then I know I need food; at other times, I seem to fade out or get extra tired. However, if my lack of sustenance doesn't obviously affect me, my family and friends know when to tell me to take a break, lie down and rest, or eat something. Usually, once I do one of these things, in no time I snap back to myself. The impact is huge as I'm a completely different person. I can go from falling asleep sitting up, to being my bright chipper self, talking a mile a minute. It is then that I am thankful that I have people watching out for me in this way.

One semester at Dean, my schedule allowed me only ten minutes between a class and tutoring. Luckily, the room I went to for tutoring was right next to the campus café. I learned to go there before tutoring to get a bagel as something to at least tide me over. When I finished tutoring, my academic coach would give me a piece of candy as an energy jolt for the rest of the afternoon. A little goes a long way.

Of course, there are so many other forms of support that I've had. I already discussed the emotional support that I needed to reinforce my belief that everything was going to be okay, but I was also reaching for academic and social support. Sometimes, it was hard to stay with my friends because they could move from place to place faster than I could or they were busy. But when I could connect with them, it was as if nothing had changed and I was still the same Marina. Realistically, I am the same Marina I was before my accident, just not physically. My friends always love hanging out with me as I do with them. We can always relate to what each other are doing. I have talked about my friends, the Greenawalts, who always make me feel special whenever I visited them.

Fast-forward a couple of years to my first full-time semester at Dean. I was in an Introduction to Theater class taught by Craig Handel, one of the college theater directors. It was a fun class and so enjoyable especially when I was first making the transition to college. Even though my high school was in a way discouraging about my future ability to participate in theater (they told my parents I would not be able to do theater in college), I still wanted to see what I could do because I'm such a strong believer that you must try before being counted out of the game. Dean was preparing to put on *Romeo and Juliet* as one of their productions. I really wanted to see what college theater would be like, so I went to the audition. I had met with Craig in class to get his perspective on what would be best for me while pursuing this. He handed me the prologue of the opening to the show. I have always been known as a drama queen because I love acting so much. A day after the audition, my Introduction to Theater class met again, and Craig wanted everyone who auditioned to recite whatever monologue they had for the whole class. I was really excited when my turn came, and Craig handed me a copy of the prologue. I read the prologue for all of them and really emphasized the wordings on the page to bring the monologue to life. I wasn't sure what everybody would think, but I still gave it my all, striving for the entire class to take away from my reading of the monologue that there was something in my heart that was even bigger than the way people perceive me.

Dean College is a great place and offered me a wonderful way to figure out life moving forward. They were the first college to accept me, and even when we told them everything negative the high school said to us, their response was, "We've got her." I was only taking two classes and still commuting back and forth from home. Nevertheless, I really began reestablishing my life in respect to needing to do things alone. People gave me so much help along the way, especially when I moved in full-time; professors, advisors, the public safety officers, and friends were always there for me to lean on or assisting me to understand where everything was. In the beginning, I had a hard time remembering where all my classes were—knowing which room and which building. It was embarrassing at the time because it seemed so easy for the other students, but now I look back and laugh at the way I took it. I remember it not being funny at the time at all, but now I can see the strides I have made when I had never been completely on my own before.

It is hard to know why some things happen. Well, maybe the ways they happen are all a part of life. Mom had taken me to a class when I was still commuting, and one of the professors had a degree in clinical psychology. She was teaching an introductory class for freshmen to help us in our adjustments. One day after class, she talked with my mom and me. We told her about everything we had heard endlessly from the high school, and she simply said, "Marina is absolutely capable of college-level work. She has to try three times harder than the other students, but she can do it." She then looked at me and said, "Marina, you are the most conscientious student in this class, and you're such a beautiful writer. Have you ever thought of pursuing anything with that?"

I had to smile at that because people had told me the same thing for years, and yet my academic liaison at the high school always said I was not capable of forming together a piece of writing on my own. That is one reason why I wrote this book. Mainly I want people to know about my struggles and how I overcame them, but also how much I have needed to stop at nothing to prove people wrong. Some limits that organizations and individuals set are heartbreaking, and I feel such a surge of confidence and joy when I surpass those limits despite struggles. I also am always hoping that more people who become aware of everything I have been through will be inspired to keep working hard, no matter what other people think or say. Everything is worth a fight, whether or not it is for a huge reward. I would never be where I am today if it weren't for all the support I've had throughout my entire life. However, I have never stopped believing in and striving for myself as well.

13

SLOWLY BUT SURELY

My accident was in 2003. Hard to believe it was that long ago.

Some of us at times expect positive outcomes to appear immediately and are upset when they don't. The issue may be progress in school or work, family life, or just things that we struggle through that frustrate them. Even with careful concentration, people can have a hard time with the simplest tasks. It took me a few years after I moved home from Spaulding before I could tie my shoes by myself. Similarly, relearning to skate and dance required more time than I expected. Occasionally my parents would take me to skate on public ice at the Skating Club of Boston on Saturdays. Of course, it was much harder for me than for others, but after going for a few weekends consistently, it got easier, and I could skate around the ice perimeter without stopping. My parents and sometimes our friends helped to keep my walker steady while I was skating. Frequently, my friends Layla and her little sister Yasmin, as well as other skating friends, happily joined me. I even was invited to come out in the finale in the Skating Club of Boston's skating show, *Ice Chips*, for two years.

One year at the Skating Club after-party when *Ice Chips* were done, another friend, Stephen Carrier, who was another skating friend I knew before my accident and didn't see often wanted to have a dance-off contest with me. That night, I really felt like a true member of that skating community again. I remember thinking that after my accident, everything would change for me. I didn't know if

I'd keep the same friends, if anyone would want to bother meeting me, or even if people would just ignore me or not listen to what I had to say. Fortunately, I was wrong about all that. If misfortune happens to a person, it's not always that they have lost the true ability to do what they love; they just must do it differently. That was a matter I had some trouble grasping at first, but now that I have hold of it, I'm happy because it assures me that doing the things I love is still possible.

One detail people sometimes do not take into consideration when there is a physical injury is muscle memory. This is a major icon in how someone will recover because if it was already in a person's brain, it is still there even after an injury. The fact is that the injured brain can't send signals as quickly or easily as that of one without an injury. I think that's one reason why I can still do these physical things. My body remembers how to dance, skate, run around, and so on. If you did it once, you can do it again. That's an important thing to remember. Even though a person is struggling with an action they used to perform well, he or she has the potential to regain it all over time. It seems to me that working hard shrinks or weakens the barrier between the brain and the body. Maybe it doesn't do that literally, but it does strengthen the weaker muscles that the person is targeting.

In my recovery, months went by slowly, but still I got better. I could use my left hand more and more for various daily tasks. Impatience gets in the way for anybody, and the heaviest burden is not knowing how long improvement will take. Over time, I have grown more understanding of this, but still it hits me straight in the heart. I get really frustrated when something isn't working for me, but when that happens, I stop, take a deep breath, and give myself a minute to get back on track. On occasion, however, I let myself give in to the frustration; if I don't allow myself to express it occasionally, it will drive me crazy, and I won't get anything done. That's not the best way to react to a problem, but everybody needs to have that kind of moment before they can let something go. When I get too apologetic for expressing a bad reaction, people tell me that if I didn't care about what happened, they would worry about me; this confirmed what Lara had told me previously too. This is always reassuring because it stops the voice in my head that is screaming at me to get it together. If I never got comfort from people in this way, I do not know where or who I would be now.

We all need to find our own strength to continue moving on. It can be hard to find especially if we have given up on hope. The only way to find it is through hard work and having patience. If we take everything day by day, we can focus on accomplishing something even if it seems unattainable at first, and at the same time, it may even be done more easily and strongly than it was before. The road to recovery in medical situations can be long, but your body gets stronger with the more effort you put into it. Even today I live by the quote by Hanu Pinyin that always hung above my bed in Spaulding: "The journey of a thousand miles begins with a single step." Anything is possible, and even if a point you want to get to seems impossible, you won't get there until you try, and trying starts with a single step. That is the kind of advice I would give to somebody in a situation similar to mine or even a person who needs to have a little push or a flicker of inspiration to keep going. Even if we are going through a difficult event, and it seems like a worst-case scenario, there is always the chance that it will improve if we give it at least the amount of effort or even more than it requires.

In some circumstances, the hardest parts are the unknown and waiting. Waiting is hard because that's when you don't know how something will turn out. There can be waiting for the world to change, waiting for violence to end. There was my family waiting to see if I would ever come out of my coma, waiting to see when I'd go home, and for me waiting for the life I knew to come back.

When people envision a goal, they often expect to accomplish it as soon as possible. However, they need to put in hard work before they can attain what they seek. Sometimes, they think a goal can be met shortly and shouldn't take extra work, should be just like walking for instance. In fact, I never was aware of how difficult and how much thought walking takes until I couldn't do it on my own. Yes, I've made miles of improvements, but I know there is so much farther I can go. Don't get me wrong, there are some days that I let myself become an emotional basket case because I remember everything from my life before getting hurt; I miss it so much that it causes an enormous pain in my heart. Until speaking to Gabe when I was fifteen, I blamed myself for having my accident and that at times made me feel even worse; I told myself it had been my decision to start riding, so I could have prevented the accident if I had not begun that avocation.

Sometimes, patience in the quest for a goal that is a painful annoyance, especially regarding some circumstances. The hardest situations is the one in which there is no defined ending point to your journey and you just have to wonder when your objective will be reached. I'm not going to lie and say it's fun, it really isn't, but if you can look at your circumstance from a different angle, perhaps you could learn something about yourself that you did not understood at first. Maybe your journey is a challenge to show people what you really can do versus what others say you can't; maybe it is to discover your calling in the world or even to set you up going in one direction and then perversely to be sent in a totally different direction from what you were planning. I have always been in theater, but now I'm also a motivational speaker. I even did my first official motivational speech to two fifth-grade classes, the teachers, my old home speech therapist, the assistant principal, and principal at Miller Elementary School in Hopkinton, Massachusetts, in 2017. Setting goals is the key to a bright future.

Since that day in April, I've had a lot of spasticity on my left side. I would get Botox vaccines to freeze the tight muscles. I most often got them in my left wrist or sometimes my left thumb for my hand and my left calf for my ankle. It was a pain to have to deal with the shots and they hurt, but now I can walk without my left ankle turning in, grasp things better, and use my left hand more. I never enjoyed getting Botox shots, but enduring them is a big reason why I'm getting better.

Doing things slowly but surely can be a simple proposition that people can overlook. It's kind of like the story about the tortoise and the hare. Slow and steady wins the race. When people think about it, they really are two different things, yet they are the same. Building muscle takes going to the gym constantly and doing slow exercises so as to obtain speed. For a few years while I was at Dean, my friend Ryan Donovan would take me to the fitness center a few times a week to work on the treadmill and other equipment. Each time I would start slowly, and Ryan would gradually increase the speed for me. After a few weeks, he would comment about my walking faster on it and showing more definition in my legs. Ryan left in 2016, so anyone who was working out in the fitness center when I was down helped me. My friends Paul or Jesse, other students, would help me to get on the treadmill, to sit at the arm machines, or just to get on to a mat on the floor to do some ab exercises. Since that time, I have been able to do more and more. There are even some instances where Lara or Mom have helped me workout at home or at the ballet studio.

Patience is not the easiest thing for many people when it comes to something they really want. All I can say is that if someone gives everything time, there is more of a likelihood of its working out. I've been in a wheelchair since I was ten, and I hate it; still I understand that I must take things bit by bit and allow time before the day comes when I don't need it. When I am down, I remember the fact that it's a miracle that I'm alive and making so much progress. I also look at everything my family and I have been told and how I've conquered it all. Being told I would never go to college or even do the same work as fellow students do was a real motivator. I was driven by it to achieve my personal best. I'm not going to say it was easy; there were so many times that I cried because I couldn't grasp concepts. I used to spend a long time on academic work because it took me longer to process information. When I finally began taking breaks after an hour or so on one piece of work, I could let it register in my brain, and in class during discussions, I understood the concepts more. Even when things don't seem as if they're going the right way at first, if people focus solely on the outcome they want, the process of the work gets lost, but if they really work through the time and effort the process requires, in most cases, anything can be attainable. I've been working on my physical and learning challenges for a very long time, but each day, I feel myself growing stronger, and I can see the light shining brighter and brighter.

14

N E V E R   G I V E   U P

Throughout this book, I constantly say don't give up. That's self-explanatory to most people, but there really is a true seriousness to it. People can never fully move on to the next step unless they truly commit themselves to the matter in front of them, whether they are struggling with something minor or dealing with more than they can handle. Regardless of what the complex problem is, they need to first identify what it is, consider what they can do about it, and finally consider alternate ways of working through it. In this way, that person understands the matter and can try out various ways of solving it.

Too many times we hear about someone giving in only because that seems like the easiest option. They may never even stop to consider if what they think is the best choice really is that or if another way of doing it might be better. Take something simple like someone struggling with a sport. That person never will become a top player unless they realize what they need to do better, evaluate how they can do it other ways, and finally use their internal data (muscle memory and past movement experience) to exert themselves in the fullest way. For instance, I was told that if I practiced the movements of skating and dancing in my head, it would help my body remember how to skate and dance. In an academic setting, a student will not master a concept they struggle with in school unless they take the time to really understand it, perhaps beyond school; this might take a little extra school work or one-on-one time with a teacher or coach to see what's wrong and speak about other strategies or ways to remember

95

tricks that simplify what the struggle is. Progress may take longer, but if a person gives up, they'll never find the answer or improve.

Often giving up may seem like an easy option. Well, it can indeed be a way to get away from problems, but it doesn't actually make them better. If people don't put in the effort to work at something, then there is no improvement and nothing that can better the future of that person. For example, if people give up on speaking professionally, then they are automatically showing that they don't care about whether they get a good job or not in the future. One has to recognize that professionalism really is an important attribute in employment and do the work to attain it.

Nobody wants to miss the chance to achieve a new position, especially if it is easy to get. Having a way to fully identify the matter at hand and how it can be solved depends on the way people see it. I know things can be accomplished if people stick to something they start and don't give up on it. The voice in your head may say, "If you're going to suffer, why bother trying?" That voice has a hard and slightly morbid way of thinking. To motivate yourself to keep going, you must learn to ignore it.

Having inspiring role models also encourages people to continue to struggle and not give up. Even children look up to good role models. For example, my siblings, Lara and Neill, are both older than I am, so I look up to them. Ever since I was little, I would watch them dance, skate, and altogether be icons for other people as well as for me. I always see them working to make their skating the best it can be. That's really what I see in them: they have a job to do, they want to do it the right way, and reach their resolution in the best way possible. Everyone who demonstrates their diligence can eventually have a positive effect on others because whatever it is they do, someone somewhere in the world wishes they had the same opportunity and may gain the motivation to strive for it.

People know that giving up is easy, but what they don't think about is the effect doing that can have on themselves and others. If you give up on something, it's really a streak where an opportunity is wasted. If you avoid deciding between two choices, you may be implying that you do not care much about what you were trying to sort out in the first place. Maybe it doesn't matter about what gets decided because you don't care if the situation is resolved or not. It may even be a matter on which a better decision is easy, if you just invest extra time and effort. Doing so, however, could also spark a new way of thinking and a new discovery. It can be hard to see how easily something can be done if you are too close to it. It is always important to be open to new perspectives and opportunities as these may be different yet easier ways to reach a desirable outcome. This again takes more time, but it's better to take more time and do something right than to do something really fast only to realize that it's all wrong.

It is always important to see a job through once it is started because it proves to yourself and others that you are stronger than you were before. Even though a project might seem impossible if it's not working at first, there is always the chance that one will see it through. This concept is hard to accept, but it is also realistic. Most people believe at some points that whatever the struggle is, they can get through it. That's true until they find out that the journey takes a lot longer than they originally thought. This recognition works as a lesson for the length of time an outcome takes, and it also serves as a reminder of what else needs to be taken into consideration for the future. Nevertheless, waiting is hard because people want the outcome they imagined right away.

Considering different perspectives offered by other people can be useful as well; if a way of doing something was successful for another person, they can pass it on so that it may help someone else. Limiting oneself to one way of solving a problem or figuring out a task is both frustrating and demoralizing. If the first path didn't work out, the effort might feel like a failure. However, when an undertaking doesn't commence as first planned, staying open-minded may provide different ways of handling it even if it means starting back at square one. We might even reach the point wanted even faster than previously expected.

Effort is the key to how much your struggle will improve. Once one commits to a venture, it is important to devote full time and effort to it. Saying that one knows something so well that one doesn't even need to try very hard is still no excuse to not give it the full amount of effort. When even the simplest thing, like a story, gets a little extra effort put into it, this alone can turn it into a high quality text that uses so much detail that a reader becomes so absorbed in the writing that they simply can't put it down. This can lead to that person becoming a new writer and best-selling author, and all they had to start with was one simple story. Sports could offer similar possibilities. After all, marathon runners may only need to start with one run a day for a few years, but with extra effort, before they know it, they are running or hand cycling in the most famous races in the world. In the same way, people grow and become more adept at mastering new concepts and physical abilities through greater exertion. Once you start a meeting or a commitment during work or any other situation, you need to give it full attention until the whole process is completed. This leads you to a more positive end result.

Everybody needs something to help them moving forward, even if it's a slight push or a bit of encouragement, to continue strengthening the aspect that is necessary for them. There is always a way to build stamina and endorsement if people allow enough time for the improvement they need. Although someone may have the desire to fulfill a job, before they can produce the outcome, they must have and use their perseverance. Along with perseverance is time. Unfortunately, people can't really judge time in an instant. We all want to, but time isn't something that anyone can visualize. By this I mean that we cannot see into the future to determine for ourselves what it will be, we just have to wait; we try our best to work as hard as possible, and we wait. In some scenarios, that is probably the hardest part for many people. We have to be strong and listen to what our conscience is telling us. We know that there's something big out there that we need to reach, but often there is a long road ahead of it. For some, it can be that they need something to believe in so that they choose the right path to take. For others, it can be as simple as finding a way to move on from a difficult period; once they move forward, they can do even more. For example, when I passed the exams in high school, I knew that my potential for getting into college was even stronger than what my family had been hearing the years before.

I'm sure that people hear this phrase a lot, but there are only a handful of people who truly live by it: nobody wants to be the person who throws everything away after an incomplete attempt. Sometimes, it can be hard to see things this way, especially if the problem is important enough to someone that they engulf themselves in so many doubts that they cannot see what can be done to solve it. Some food for thought in this context can be that people need to really understand what they are getting themselves into through the decisions they make.

15

L E T ' S   S E E   H O W
F A R   I ' V E   C O M E

I'm not going to say any part of this has been easy, it hasn't. Sometimes, I let my emotions out; it is not healthy to hold them in all the time, so sometimes, I let them go. It makes me feel better instead of letting the feelings well up inside me until they burst out of me. I used to get mad at myself for getting so upset on occasion, but my family always tells me that if I didn't care or get emotional at times, then I would not have the same driven attitude that I do. There have been so many times where when I do get upset about it, I just look back on what people tell me about the time in the hospital.

There are times when I try to reach back and remember what my family has told me about those months in the hospitals. Although there are some things I want to know, I have to be careful about who I ask. I know nobody in my family wants to remember that horrible time, so I try not to ask them. What I do remember is that it was literally a living nightmare that I couldn't wake up from. I was stuck under that sheet of ice, and no matter how hard I would push, I couldn't break free. When I think about it more, I debated with myself sometimes whether I really want to know or not.

When I occasionally let myself break down, it is a good opportunity for me to reflect. Each time I remember the dark days, I am beyond thankful to be alive. My doctors at Boston Medical Center would tell my parents that if I had gotten hurt that badly ten years before, I would not have survived. Letting go of all my stressors and frustrations makes me feel so much better because it releases my internal constrictions. Even today, people tell me that I'm an inspiration to them. It actually took me some time to understand their reasoning, but then I look back on everything I do now, and I know.

Looking back, I can see how even the simplest things make a world of difference. When I was in rehab at Spaulding, I was mainly put on the standing boards before walking and walked using the parallel bars or walked with my physical therapist. When I first started therapy, I wasn't walking well, and I was getting really tired going a short distance. When I progressed to outpatient therapy, I went from walking on the parallel bars to walking with the quad cane. Looking back, those little accomplishments made the biggest progression.

If I had not fought so hard to snap out of my coma and get my stability back, I wouldn't be where I am now. Similarly, if my body had just given in to the coma, my brain wouldn't have started healing, and I would not be alive today. If I had not kept trying, I wouldn't have left the rehab hospital for even longer than the five months I spent there. However, my recovery would not have been as successful as it was if it were not for the motivation and support I had gotten from other people.

I think about how long it has been since I got hurt, and I think back to what my doctors said to my family: that I was unlikely to survive and that if I did, I would not be able to wake up from my coma or be able to interact with people again. Though it is frustrating to think of how hard I had to work, I have turned it into the motivating factor that I talked about earlier. Sometimes, frustration does get the better of me, but I do believe that's what helped my drive and determination. When my parents and I go out, sometimes I see people stare at me as they walk by; this used to drive me crazy, but over time, I've turned that into another motivator. I've started believing that they were looking at me because they were impressed because I had worked so hard. Even today people have come up to me saying what a great job they were seeing me do. That's the best feeling, knowing that people see hard work and they appreciate it.

Even with schooling, I see an enormous difference. My parents were told that I would not learn past the fourth-grade level, but then

I made it to college. I have also been through only being able to walk short distances without getting tired, to achieving miles of distances with consistent stamina. Sometimes, I wonder what could have been if I hadn't fought so hard and if I had not had so much motivation and determination. This is a difficult thing to try to imagine because reliving the experience is a horror itself. I don't remember what happened, but from everything I hear about from friends and family, it's been pretty clear how awful the whole thing was. Everybody needs something from their past that encourages them to keep trying whatever the struggle is. It is the best way, especially if they are at the last resort before giving up on everything.

With success always comes a journey. The original situation defines the level of work someone really needs to produce. With most goals comes a long series of attempts that are a result of the outcome that someone either achieves or fails.

People don't always get all of what they want on the path to achieving their goal. I was always hoping for things to change in such a way that I could live the way I remember. I can see that some things are harder than anyone wants them to be. However, people need to understand that some things just take time. I know that over time, I have attained various triumphs in my life that many people had previously doubted I would reach. People need to approach life slowly, and then they will know what really is achievable regarding anything that takes effort. The surgeries I've had make all the difference in my abilities now. If it were not for my pump surgery, I might not be walking as much, smoothly, or easily as I am now. I still need assistance from either someone else or some device, but either way, my walking has improved tremendously. That said, there is still a lot of improvement to work on. Even some places my family and I travel are challenging too. Some places aren't completely accessible and require more work for me to get through and for others to help me through. Some things may not be happening as quickly as I want them to, but little by little, they are coming.

Prediction of the future can be hard to accept sometimes. None of us liked what my family and I had been told, about how my future would look. In some cases, I had to listen to people who would offer me a distressing opinion of how something might be. I always took what is said and try my best to overcome it. Sometimes, I need help from my friends or family to help keep me on the right track. If someone would tell me they thought I would have to repeat a test in school before even giving me the chance to do it, I would try my best but sometimes not get a good grade. Instead of getting upset with myself and admitting I just couldn't do it, I would take whatever the outcome was, work harder and longer, and I would really focus when it was time for the next test. With all that, I usually did better than before. When I took economics at Dean the spring of 2015, this class was very complex, and I didn't know if I could really pass it. My grade was low in the beginning of the spring, but as the semester went on, I would meet with the professor to understand concepts better, and I began studying with two friends from my class as well. I think that effort really helps in turning your standing around.

For example, when I was ready for graduation in the spring of 2015, prior to getting my associate's degree, I received an important email from Academic Affairs. It said that because of my GPA I was eligible to write, submit, and audition a speech as the associate's graduate at graduation. Of course, after viewing this email, I was mentally jumping for joy and already thinking about what I would write. I had to tell my tutor right away. I waited a few days to give myself time to fully take it all in and sort out what else I could say to her. Then one afternoon after my classes, I pulled out a piece of paper where I had written some notes and couldn't resist starting a draft. When it was done, I read through it again and again, made some more edits, read it to some other people to get their opinions, and a few days later went down to the audition where I read it to the graduation committee.

I was so excited but also hadn't thought I'd need to read it to a group of people. I stood up to read it to them, and I could tell they liked it. A few weeks later, I received an email giving their selection of who would read for both degrees. I wasn't selected to read at the ceremony, but that did not upset me. It was disappointing, but then I could see it from the perspective that I was given the opportunity to write a speech, and further, I was a finalist to audition it in front of the committee. Either way, it was a big accomplishment to even be given that amount of a chance. It also was very reassuring because this was another factor that meant I was proving myself as a writer, not only to a few professors, but also to the school board as a whole. Also, thinking back to the fact that my high school was constantly telling my parents that I was not capable of writing correctly on my own, writing and auditioning a graduation speech was proving myself as a writer and proving to myself that I could write a really good speech for the college.

There were other ways I was able to track my physical progress through life. Lara creates YouTube skating videos that she sends out to skating show companies when she is trying to audition for a show. She combines various photos and some video clips, strings them together, puts them to music, and makes them into a video. After years of watching her do this, I finally did one myself. In high school, whenever we had our plays, our theater teacher and director, Richard Weingartner, always played a specific song for us. This was "Don't Give Up" by Eagle Eye Cherry as a reminder of the theater ensemble as a family and the need to never leave anyone in the darkness. Of course, I couldn't help making my first video to this specific song.

The video consisted of encouraging sayings, a video clip from the skating competition that happened the week before my accident, photos from sports camp, working out in the gym at Dean, a picture just as I was coming out of my coma, a clip from the video of the dance to 'Simple Gifts' I did with Lara and Neill, another clip of me on a rowing machine from a tryout for Paralympics in college, a high school graduation photo, and ending the project, a video of me walking with my cane all by myself at Goose Rocks one year and ends with a quotation, "If you feel like giving up, just look at how far you are already."

This entire video is a fabulous way to view aspects of my life both before and after my accident. I did not know how to make a video on the computer by myself, so my friend, Amanda, did it with me one day when she was at my house. We had a few things to start it with; five hours later, we had a beautiful inspirational video, which I titled "Hard Work Pays Off." I get nostalgic whenever I see it because it is replaying my whole life story in a brief period of time.

In order to maximize my confidence about staying with something I have begun, I decided to make a second inspirational video. After Lara and I had come home from the second year of Brainfarmers, somebody from camp posted on the camp Facebook page the song "Fight Song" by Rachel Platten, which has become a massive hit. After a few weeks, I had another idea for a video. I found another inspirational quotation, added the same video clip from my skating competition, a photo from *The Nutcracker*, a picture of me receiving my associate's degree at graduation in 2015, one of my family, and finally a photograph of me windsurfing. In the same way, I put all the pieces together, set it up to "Fight Song," and began playing it for myself. When all was said and done with it, Dad was able to help me change the pitch of the song, and we posted the video on YouTube and Facebook. In no time, people started liking and commenting on it. I was so happy to watch my own story develop through the videos as they both were showing significant contributions to where I was and how much improvement I have made over time. That being said, this video I titled none other than "I Can Do It."

Through watching both of these videos, I can see how much improvement I have really made from where I was; they also encouraged me to keep going if I feel defeated or my situation really starts annoying me. As much as I try to push these feelings aside, sometimes I can't help reacting to them. Sometimes, I have a hard time seeing my improvements because I'm the one working so hard. The videos help to remind me that when I try something again and again, it gets easier from the perspective of rehearsal and muscle memory. I can walk easily when I have enough support, and it only gets better the more I practice at it. Everything takes some level of a fight, but if one never gives up on the job they have to do, the fight to the finish is usually worth all the effort.

When I think about the time following my accident, I remember that I was at first so angry about things that had become much harder. I still miss everything I did in my life before, but I feel like that helps my drive. I remember what it was like to run around with my friends, and since I want that back, it makes me work harder physically. If other people can make such a difference in the world through what they do, why can't I? The memories I still have only help my determination to get my physical mobility back, and I'm not giving up on a journey that I've already worked so hard to get through.

When I look back at my abilities prior to the accident, everything comes back to me. I remember what it was like to run around, skate, dance; I still have all the feeling of those movements, so that helps when I try to go back to any of them. Each physical motion has its own place in my brain and my heart. Since I already had done it, the concept and production of movement is better and more likely than it would be if I didn't already know the feeling. I can do everything I did before, I just need more help and to do it differently. (Unfortunately, there are some activities for which I have no previous memory; those are harder.) My ability to make use of my memories has become a very encouraging way for me to think about it because it is a reminder that everything is still there, and it lets me keep on believing that I am getting closer and closer to its coming back.

The whole thought process that people faced that were frightening challenges to go through can be heartbreaking and scary all at the same time. I find I need to deal with fear in any situation that it approaches me. Most people, if they have too much fear, avoid doing whatever it is that is scary for them. As for me, I'm altogether not afraid of anything anymore. When I think about it, I have been through a literal living nightmare like I said earlier; it's a miracle that I'm still alive, and I'm still working very hard regardless of everything else. In order to make it through a really hard challenge, sometimes being fearless is the only way to go. People can say they are fearless, but they can only determine that when they actually go through something challenging. Being fearless is—or isn't—how someone approaches an action in life. Determining if one is fearless is not a fun thing. One has to prove that they can make it through an unfortunate circumstance and have the same self-confidence to do it again. No one likes having to confront a negative situation more than once. It can be even worse if it becomes more consistent. I am sometimes in a position in which something happens to a friend, and, being the way I am, I can't help but dive in and do whatever I can to help them. It has gotten easier for me to reach out to them the more times I do so, and most of the time, whatever I say to them seems to help them more than I thought it would. When I meet a person confronting a frightening situation, and I think that based on my own experience I can help, I feel compelled to ask and have more confidence in my value, to myself and others, than I once did. Even today, I look back and can see how much farther I have come from where I was and how much my advisory and physical skills have grown.

When I look back on the past, it all seems surreal to me. I have done so many things that other people would not get the opportunity to do. If I hadn't sustained my accident, I might not have become such a motivational and inspirational person. I might never have become so close to AccesSportAmerica, Zeno Mountain Farm, Love Your Brain, Access to Theater, the Katie Lynch Foundation, and in general would not be the person who I am today.

16

TRUTH BE TOLD

Every time a person questions something, they need to think about what's really possible. We all know that hard work is the key to achieving any goal. Along the way, it is important to remember to be true to oneself and one's purpose. Nothing can be achieved if a person gives up and does not bother putting out the effort to work toward a desired end. Giving up on a goal one has been trying to attain is just an easy escape for those who don't put in the amount of effort it requires. People who don't try for an objective will never reach it and will forever live in a mystery of what if because they never saw it through. Still the truth can be a heavy burden depending on what it is. Sometimes, people fear finding the truth in a matter because they worry that the answer might not be the one that they want.

A given person may have a lot they need to search for before finding the truth. Searching for it can also be troublesome because it can reveal that they have a long road ahead of them. One truth I was facing was the road to recovery. My family and I all thought I would have my physical life back in no time, but I'm still in a wheelchair most of the time because my balance sometimes goes off. I can walk but not completely independently. The hardest part of the struggle I've had to deal with on the road to recovery, as I mention a lot, has been waiting. Unfortunately, through all my hard work, I need to keep in the back of my mind that I will never know the point I can get to unless I keep working while waiting for the progression to blossom.

There are many ways to discover the truth for oneself, but discovering the truth has to be through all the work one puts into the journey. People embarking on that journey need to be strong and not let what other people say define them. This perspective has to be achieved through drive and assertive determination, to stick with what they really want, whether or not really believing they can get there. Nobody knows what really can be done without trying. Through trying, seekers can see for themselves if the process they are intending to follow is really a worthwhile way of approaching their journey. Others can predict what they think the outcome of a situation will be, but no one can really know what it is exactly until they try it and see for themselves. No one should ever assume something is true because there is always the chance that it will turn around. Sometimes, when a person is afraid of finding out what an outcome really will be, they don't bother going the extra mile to see what else they can do about it.

The truth is not always an easy thing to accept. Especially if the truth isn't to your satisfaction, accepting it becomes even harder. That's where people just need to push what others say aside and try to reach their own way to find their truth.

The truth can be a harder concept than people think. It can be both extremely hard to find and also emotionally difficult to accept. If a person really wants something that they know they can't get, it is hard for them to accept because of how much they desire it. In the same way that it can be hard to find, the truth can also be hard to grasp hold of. In this instance, people can find truth, but they sometimes have trouble holding on to it, perhaps allowing other people's doubts to diminish their confidence in themselves or their process of getting back to what they believe they are really capable of.

People strive to learn what they really can do all through their lives. After all, it's so much better than having an unanswered question all our lives. Well, sometimes the truth hurts, other times it takes a long time to find, but in some situations, it leads you to the answer you want. For me, the truth has been hard to reach and I'm not quite there yet, but I keep working hard because I can see it in the distance. Either way it works out. When a person reaches the answer they were searching for, it is as if a heavy weight is lifted off them. If one didn't work toward a goal they had envisioned, it might never be achieved simply because that person didn't put in the amount of effort it takes. Goals can be an icon that people worship or they can be a nemesis to annoy them; sometimes, it can be both. It can be seen this way: I talked early on about seeing a point people want to reach; this point may represent the truth, and where seekers end up going, with the required amount of work, usually leads them to the desired outcome. That's what I mean when I say, "Be told." Just put these two phrases together and the answer is simple. Find something you want to achieve, work hard at it, and there is more of a chance that you will achieve the desired answer you want. Truth be told.

17

SHE'S COMING BACK

Whenever I really think back to my life before getting hurt, I have a very wistful feeling. I remember where I was, and I miss it! Sometimes even now, I continue to feel frustrated that I have been working so hard and still am not where I want to be yet.

I would try to see beyond the way friends of mine had been moving on in ballet, skating, or even classes at school, but in the back of my mind, there still was something nagging at me. In school, I would take tests and would see people from my classes get out within maybe twenty minutes; meanwhile, I was only halfway through. Sometimes, I watched friends running around with each other or playing a sport out on the field while I just sat on the side and watched. Eventually though, I learned that whenever I would compare myself to others, I could stop myself and try to think about something else. Comparing really doesn't do any good.

Further, I started figuring out other ways to participate in activities even if I could not physically play. I taught myself to analyze the movement I was watching and imagine ways to improve it. As I was observing a skating class, I noticed that a friend was having trouble landing one of her jumps. I suggested to her something that might help, after which she was able to land the jump. Similarly, a friend who was cast as "Paris" in a production of *Romeo and Juliet* read some of his lines for me. After listening closely, I suggested that he pause before giving the final line, a change that he agreed improved the speech. He recited his lines again, used the pause, and he sounded perfect. In such ways, I was able to feel involved and could provide real benefits to friend as well.

Each day, one has to see some sort of positivity emerging in one's life. When I was studying at Dean, I attended an event in which we all designed our own hat to be spray-painted by a visiting artist. I chose to have my hat painted in pink, purple, and blue, my three favorite colors, and requested that the artist print on the front the phrase, "Each day counts." The reason I chose these words aligns with what I believe in: never give up. It really is important to look at life that way. Our days in the world are numbered; they can be taken away at any moment. No matter what is going on in our lives or the world, we have to cherish each day while we still can. No one wants to go through life always regretting something they've experienced as if it were a waste. Whether the experience really was a negative point in one's life or not, whatever anyone endures makes them a stronger person. Sometimes, we have a choice in that, other times we don't. I see the gifts in life more than its difficulties, and I don't want to waste any moments if I can help it.

I see where I am now, and, yes, some things are different. I still can't get up and walk on my own, but every day, I feel myself growing stronger. I think back to the days in the hospitals, and I already know I am much farther along compared to where I was. Listening to all the negativities people have directed at me has been really discouraging, but it also helped me become who I am today, and knowing what I have done that people said I couldn't do is a very rewarding feeling. Further, I can never forget the cheering squad I've had behind me. If I ever begin doubting myself, they are always there helping to push me forward. Sure, I'm still not where I want to be, but I can see the light, and now I just have to complete my reach for it.

Be that as it may, I have had a really hard emotional recovery process from my accident. Physically, I know I'm limited, but I still try my best and can get a lot accomplished. When I hear the word limit, I just laugh. I know I have some limits right now, but as long as I work hard enough, I can slowly but surely decrease and eventually even eliminate them. It's not that any of this is easy (believe me, it's not), but it also parallels the challenges life throws at us. Even today, my family, friends, and doctors become emotional when they look at me because they remember that I was in such bad shape for a really long time.

Yes, challenges can be a pain to deal with at the time, but a person who confronts them becomes so much stronger. A small effort can go a long way. If someone accomplishes something small, like taking a few steps, they might think nothing of it; later on, however, they may find out that what they did has made such a big difference that people all over the world are inspired to attempt the same thing and achieve similar results. People need to keep an eye out for anything that can help or an opportunity to say or create something that is beneficial toward a wide variety of people. I had my accident and, after waking up from my lengthy coma, found out people all over the world were praying for me.

Accepting the difficulty of a horrendous situation is not the most attractive option as the circumstance really is painful, especially when the objectives is so much harder to work toward than either one's self or others expected, but it is needed nonetheless. I think about everything I've already done and where I've come from, regardless of what people tell me. I always appreciate it when I meet someone who doesn't know about my story but finds my words moving as they speak with me. As I explain in further detail what I've been through, I start becoming even more confident in myself than I was the minute before. I start recapping my life, and from there, I can really see a correlation between my words and who I am now.

When people have injuries, there are different outcomes, as I've said before. Some people in recovery become people far from who they were before their injury. Others might show attributes that are somewhat different from what they used to be. Some of the people I knew at Spaulding experienced massive changes from who they were before, whether being outgoing where they used to be quiet and shy or the other way around. As for me, even though I was so badly hurt, I'm still the same Marina I always was. I still love being around people, cheering them on and cracking jokes. If someone is upset, I can cheer them up with my sense of humor too. There have been times when if I have been sad or angry, I stop and think for a minute and then out of nowhere burst out laughing. Sometimes, people even turn to look at me because often I laugh to the point where I can't breathe. That's another reason why I'm not completely resentful of everything that happened to me in 2003. I can shake off a lot of things because I can cheer myself up so that I stop thinking about it, and, of course, the fact that I am surrounded by friends and family who all make me happy is an immense help.

Over the years, I have gone out of my way to strive for things that help me get back to those spontaneous times I had. Instead of focusing on what I couldn't do on my own, I would concentrate on what I could.

I became part of an adaptive crew team when I was in high school. I worked harder with AccesSportAmerica to improve my windsurfing skills, running, walking, and soccer. I spent time at Mom's ballet studio and even choreographed my own adapted dance for my parents before I graduated from high school. I've come so far from where I first started following the accident. There are ways to do the old things I loved; they just have to be done differently.

Now people see me not as the girl in the wheelchair but as a strong, determined, and committed person because each day I feel as if, compared to where I was before, I'm getting closer and closer to reaching my desired result. Friends and family even notice my determination because they see me trying again and again. They also see my drive to reach that point that has always been so far off in the distance. I always feel as if I'm meant to do something or to make a difference in communities all over the world. Every day I can see that possibility becoming clearer and clearer. The sky is the limit!

Every time I make even the smallest improvement, it makes the biggest difference. When I was in my coma, both my family and my doctors were overjoyed when I finally began making noises, which slowly evolved into words. After that, people could actually believe I had a chance to fully wake up. It's funny how just one little action can turn into such a big difference. People had seen where I had been before the accident; they wanted me back, and now they knew that I could get there. Slowly, I continued improving more and more.

That pattern of improvement continued through my high school and college years. As a student at Dean, I began using the treadmill more and more, had an easier time keeping my feet from turning in, using my time in school to my benefit, allowing myself to be a part of more groups and social settings in school, and in general finding my own way to go through life. People wonder who I would have been if nothing had happened to me. I wonder that sometimes myself. When that happens, sometimes I get upset, wishing I could do everything physically that I did before. That's when I realize that I really can do pretty much what I did before. It's all just a lot harder.

People sometimes use the excuse that they are too busy to work at something. I hear that and just shake my head. Everything has to be worked for in some way. If a goal is truly important, it needs a lot of time and effort put into it. Maybe things are hard at the time, but if people keep their head up, then they are already inviting the possibility for what they really want to actually come about.

Having faith and leading a person on with false hope are not the same things at all. Superficial encouragement of the person who faces a significant challenge may be well-meant but is not really helpful. Having faith, on the other hand, means understanding what the striving person wants and acknowledging that the road to their goal may be difficult to travel but that it's possible to get there.

Now I know what it is like to fight for what you believe in. I've been fighting to walk independently again, and I believe I can get there. It is important to remember my life before the accident but also to keep my mind open to new actions and opportunities life can offer, whether it is an opportunity someone thinks may be out of reach for me or something that can be seen in my future. My family and friends love being with me, and in some ways, we feel as if everything is the same as it used to be. They notice every little new detail that is an improvement in the way I can do a task independently. I used to need someone to help me to stand up, but now I can get myself up from the floor to standing with only the help of a cane.

As I describe what I remember from my time in the hospital, I look at it in the context of the improvement I've made coming from where I was. It can mean all the difference when one can listen to people, even those who suggest that progress will be limited but still go one's own way. Regardless of what someone goes through, whether it is a tragedy, accident, discovery, or even something that is crucial as a high, exciting point in life, people have to work hard to achieve what they want. As for me, my goals are never-ending, and my determination is still growing at a mile a minute. In real life, even when people struggle through something that seems as if it will never change, the reality is that it might be able to; they just have to really commit themselves to extra amounts of work so that they can reach a desired point even if it still seems hazy in the distance.

I know that things are different for me right now, but I believe in possibilities, maybe even to the extent that I seem a little too optimistic. However, I feel it's better to believe in too much in order to get to a higher level than it is to give up. People see me differently today from a physical aspect, but once they actually get to know me, they see how comfortable I am, how much I love socializing, and if they have known me before getting hurt, they can see all the same attributes I had as a very young person. They realize that maybe the new Marina is in fact the same person that could run across the grass on her own, race the whole school outside on the field, or challenge all the boys on the basketball court. Day by day, little by little, she's coming back.

18

ANYTHING IS POSSIBLE

Struggles are hard for anybody to deal with. Whether or not solving a problem seems realistic, succeeding or failing at it is all based on the way you decide to see the task through. That can be the defining factor in how much confidence the person has. Whenever people have an objective that they want to obtain, regardless of the way they feel, it is up to their level of encouragement, drive, and self-confidence to determine if their goal is reachable. The circumstance may involve difficult actions for them to play out, but difficulty even adds to the importance of where they reach in the end.

There is a persistent internal conflict with the sense that there is always something that can hold us back and keep us from moving on. Sometimes, it can be small and easy to push through, but other times it is so big that it clouds a person's mind so fully that they can see nothing but the failure even before completing the job. Even when the situation seems really overwhelming and doesn't seem to make sense, hard work is the motor that pushes us through the boundaries that had seemed so impenetrable. Everybody needs to know that no matter what they are struggling with, there is usually a chance that it will get better. Often, people assume that things are impossible, so they don't even try. Sometimes, it is perfect timing to realize how important something is, but on other occasions, it might only seem to be too late to accomplish something by the specific amount of time available. For instance, I haven't been where my doctors thought I would be mobility-wise, but I just keep hanging on, working as hard as I possibly can; I don't know if my mobility will come fully back, but I want to see how far I can get with the work I put into it.

Obviously being doubted and put down by people who barely know me is beyond annoying, but I also still take it as a motivational factor to see where I can go. Anytime I feel defeated by something I can't do, I think about whether there's a way I can do it a little differently. Over the years, I have learned how to adapt things so that they are still possible for me to do. I have been exposed to many different standards of judgment from people saying that they didn't think I would get far in life to others who saw me doing great things in the future. People hear about events coming down in the world, sometimes not in the way we want. When this comes about, it is important to separate what one imagines life should be versus what is rational when it comes to the feasible resolution of that situation.

There have been times when everything seems like it's in darkness; whereas if people hold on a little tighter, or for even a second longer, it works out. In this situation, just a little encouragement or understanding from another person can make all the difference. Even the suggestion of something that seems like a last resort or an idea that appears as if it wouldn't help at all, no matter what it is, may be useful; if someone takes a little time to express that issue, it can make all the difference in one's ability to resolve the problem. I have been in situations where I put a lot of effort into what might be a simple suggestion to someone else, but then it helps them tremendously. I'm always happy when it works out this way for them both because not only I have helped someone with something they can't figure out on their own but also because it gives me the feeling that people really benefit from some of the advice and ideas I bring to them.

Possibilities in themselves are really a precious thing. Recognizing them shows that we have a bit of confidence in ourselves and reflects what we have already done and what is truly possible. All through life, people endure halts that seem to stop time. These can occur at any moment for us, sometimes at the worst moments or situations. Either way, this can also be seen as a good thing because they are the substance of what we overcome. Even if it doesn't happen often, everybody needs to know how to accept the existence of these obstacle. That's not saying they should be accepted as a done deal, but we need to allow them to enter into us as a catalyst so that we can accelerate something inside that can possibly overtake them. It's not an easy metaphor to understand at first glance, but it is crucial to testing the self-defense mechanism that can get the intruders out. It's easier to take in when we think about what really can help us right then and there. Every day, people go through a battle between allowing negative thoughts to drive into their heads and shoving them out by thinking about positive attributes that can really help them. Desperate times call for desperate measures, which means that if somebody really needs help with something, they have to seek out the best type of treatment, ways to defend themselves or somebody else. Halts get in our way, but it is up to us whether they keep us from getting through to a solution that we need.

There are times where we all act against what our full potential is. Life is all about the journey to find out who we are and what our place is. We have to approach everything one step at a time instead of charging through to the finish line, which is what most people seem to want. We may see our finish line in the distance, but that is just the beginning of the journey because it is what we want, but we need to strive for it. People say that they can get somewhere without trying the amount that is actually required. Well, again, easier said than done. We are all human, and we all have goals for ourselves. That alone shows that we believe in possibilities and that we are sure we can get there. It doesn't matter what is holding us back, whether it is ability, confidence, lack of support, or even what we perceive of ourselves. True, we have to keep an open and unclouded mind about where we are at a given point, recognizing that things may be harder for us than for another person, but as important as it is to keep your mind rationally open, you always need to keep your head up, push forward, and take everything one step at a time. This way, you can achieve anything even beyond what you thought was possible.

This kind of attitude might seem hard to stick with or even accept. Depending on the situation we're in, being patient and staying positive is the hardest thing because we feel as if it's not what we really want. I have been in the position where I get upset because I've felt that my mobility should be in a better place now. It's natural to feel this way, and it is healthy because it has helped to show me where I needed to work harder. There's a point where the world seems like everything's going wrong and we feel desperate in our times of need. This is where that glimmer of faith can grow even with the smallest amounts of effort we put in.

We all want things to go right in our lives. Before doing something right, sometimes it has to be wrong. This is the best way to learn what works and what doesn't. Thinking about how things can be done another way leads us to follow different paths, and afterward, we might have discovered another way something will work. That in turn can then show people new ways tasks can be completed. An example of this could go back to when I walked at my high school graduation. I needed to have both my friend Caleb and the physical therapist to spot me in case I stumbled. This way, the responsibility wouldn't have to be all on Caleb in case that happened. Thankfully, it didn't.

Nobody knows right away if something will really be worth the effort they put in or not. That's the reason they need to try, no matter what the challenge might seem like at first. I've heard from Mom this best example of the reason, "If you don't try, you're guaranteed not to know." This is a phrase I have always lived by because it's so true. If something seems hard but we want to try to overcome it, we will never know the answer to that unless we actually treat it as the challenge it is and see for ourselves whether we can conquer it or not. We might not get it the first time, but that's where we can discover different strategies and ways of seeing it through.

There is always something to look forward to in our lives, regardless of those problems that stopped us for a moment. The objective we look forward could be something which we want to work toward, something to help other people, maybe even something else that can be of future impact in our lives. Having a goal or a role model is great for us because it gives people an ideal to work toward or be as good as, whether it seems reachable for them or not. Nobody can determine where someone else could go in life because it has to be the responsibility of every person to commit to determining the future for themselves.

Not knowing our future is only half the battle. That's just the question that we want answered. Like it or not, getting our answer also requires patience. Sometimes, the process needs to be taken with caution and baby steps. Further, the time we take shouldn't be seen as time wasted or as too long, but rather it should be considered as the time we commit to our work, whether it is physical, mental, academic, or emotional. This uncertainty about an unknown future can lead to the stressors that undermines our confidence even if it seems like we are in a good place.

So many things were different back in 2003. It was a hard year for a lot of people, not just me. I still question where the time goes, why some improvements come faster than others; I still wonder where the days go and question why inexplicable things happen in the world. Nobody can go through life assuming how things will be and expecting fate will always work out in their favor. When life does not seem to be working the way we want, we need to keep believing every day that there is a possibility for the situation to improve. I think back to that day in 2003, and I know it has actually helped me develop into the stronger, more assured, independent person that I am today; that would never have happened if that dreadful occurrence had never come to my riding lesson. There is a silver lining in most situations; what matters is just what we do to allow ourselves to see it. We all have to keep believing in what is possible. Even in our darkest times, when things seem really rough, we must keep in the back of our minds that anything is possible because it is. Struggles may cloud our visions for a while, but if we can all push past the darkness, we might just reach that light we see off in the distance.

19

RESPONDING TO DOUBTERS

Everything comes with a price, whether that is falling constantly while playing sports or getting headaches from studying for long periods of time; sometimes, it is wise to take a break to focus on another activity and returning to your work refreshed. There is something to be said for making that sort of choice and using it to our advantage.

Most people want to have their sights set on something eventually, and it is that person's responsibility to determine how to see it through. When given a hard time, many people's automatic response is to push back and defend themselves. Negative reinforcement can actually be the best form of positive reinforcement sometimes. It sounds confusing at first, but really when people are told they can't do something, the initial response is that they want to prove that person wrong. This usually leads to their working harder and harder.

Needless to say, this is how I approach this issue all the time. When someone doubts me, I don't say this out loud, but mentally, I'm saying, *Oh, yeah? Watch me.*

Once when I was talking to a woman about where I thought I was at in my abilities, I told her about my goal of walking at my high school graduation. She said she wasn't sure if I'd really be able to do that. I cleverly responded as my usual determined and motivated self, "Then I'll run."

This is one of the reasons I recovered the way that I did. People can say whatever they want, but really what they express is just their opinion. It's always up to you, the subject person, to accept what is said or to explore and follow your own way. Having people to back you up provides one of the best chances at whether the other person believes you. This statistic can be innumerable. If you seem to be making progress against the odds, against what other people predict, you may start a full trend. Others in difficult positions may be inspired to follow the way in which you proactively took charge of the circumstances. Letting others who lack factual evidence control your future diminishes the chance of evoking similar responses from others. None of us would then find the answers we want.

Some people might believe that there could be a point at which they need to stop what they're doing without finishing and still not be disappointed. Well, from my experience, if someone works hard at a task and then stops suddenly, never returning to it, they may actually feel as if all their work was wasted. That said, sometimes people need to take breaks so that they don't overwhelm themselves with the matter at hand. This happens even when we least expect it. It still happens to me today, and I just need to stop, think, and proactively try a different way to complete the work. None of this is easy to deal with, but in a real sense, difficulty is what makes people stronger. Though it seems like a heavy burden for us, it shows others how committed we are to improving.

I have already covered a lot of the extraneous background noise derived from what people say regarding my situation. If we believe in ourselves and have the proper drive required in order to keep moving on, no one can control the results besides ourselves. Some people are open to embracing new ideas and ways of thinking about how to best manage a situation, but others might only want to proceed with them according to their own way of thinking. This difference between various people's ways of approaching a situation can put them and everyone else in a complicated scenario: half of the people think they know rationally what to do, but the other half wants to do it their own more instinctive way. I have always believed that if someone adheres strongly enough to their intuition, with more and more hard work, they can see their goals through to the way they want.

Even if there is a question as to what is yet to come, we all need to use our own inner strength to get through whatever obstacle is in our way. For me, high school was a really challenging time when I had to prove myself as a learner. When there were doubts about my learning and exam-taking capabilities, I was put to the test and really started to understand how to go about producing the work that teachers wanted and using knowledge gained from past experience to tackle other issues in school. There had been questions about my ability to handle participating in the school theater ensemble as it involved a more concentrated level of work, but I was able to manage it even when people said I couldn't.

It's never fun to listen when someone else is disparaging one's capabilities. We need to remember that the doubting person may be using personal judgments as opposed to what really could be a result if nothing else is standing in the way. In my case, it seemed that no matter what I did to prove them wrong, some people still couldn't see the light.

The opinions of doubters actually can cause a burden at times. If they insert so much negativity into another person's life, it is possible that they can eliminate any chance for a positive outcome. My advice to people when it comes to this is stated throughout this book. Whenever someone doubts you, don't listen to them and keep trying your own way. After all, no one can determine your capability completely except you. This is frustrating at times especially when you are working so hard (as I have said), but realistically, the only thing standing in the way between you and a desired point to get to is yourself. That's not to put anyone facing a challenge down who reads this text, but it's just telling the truth of how hard getting through a journey may be. Just remember, you can always take what someone says and actually use it to your own advantage. Then you can see that doubt doesn't have to be just a negative way to look at your current situation.

At some point in our lives, we all face an idea or action that we question. This strengthens our idea of what we think we are capable of ourselves. What other people think is just an opinion. It's up to us to see through that distraction. If we let it overtake us, then we are giving in to that attitude before finding out if its judgment is true or false. Many of us question our place in the world at times, for instance. However, we will never discover what our place truly is or could be if we give in to the doubts people impose on us or judge from what they see superficially. We might mistakenly question something just because of others' views and opinions. If I had given in to the doubts of everyone, I probably wouldn't have been so successful in college, in sports, or even be alive.

The most critical words when it comes to doubt are "if" and "yet." None of us wants to live with a question that we could never answer: what if?

What if something doesn't work out in my favor? What if I'm just not good enough? What if I can't do it?

Even instead of expressing frustration that where we are isn't what we want yet, we need to be patient.

"Okay, I'm not there yet." "It hasn't worked out yet."

Patience is sometimes the hardest thing, especially depending on the amount of time we spend waiting. The only thing to do is try our hardest and do whatever we can to charge through to the outcome we want. With all the frustration that comes around, in order to stay positive, we need to start using the word "yet." "I'm not there yet." It shows that there is still a possibility for the improvement to come in time.

Doubt is like that thing that we try to block out of our minds, but it still follows us wherever we go. It's almost always seen as a negative thing in that if we doubts sufficiently, we are giving up on any chance for it to work out. Only if we use the doubt instead of always trying to shut it away can we help ourselves discover alternative ways to successfully accomplish something. Nobody likes to doubt themselves, and we all want answers to our questions. The only thing we can do, regardless of what others think, is to go ahead and follow our minds and hearts. If we listen too much to what others say, that can really invade our heads and possibly push whatever thought which motivated us before out of our mind. We have to push through our fear and advance with an open mind. Only then will we find that answer. Maybe it won't be the answer we want, but then again, maybe it will; now we are taking it in and seeing it through.

Trying to explore something unknown is better than doing nothing at all and not knowing. That's just where we all need to believe that it will get better. Yes, we all wish problems wouldn't arise and that we don't have to go through the pain of going to so much trouble to figure conflicts out, but everything that challenges us makes us that much stronger. We never know how much something can benefit us until we give it a try, and the starting point to get there is if we believe we can.

People base many things on what they have done in the past. This can represent what we know we can do, which jump-starts our senses, which encourages us to try something again and again. Maybe it won't work out the way we want, but there is also a chance that it can. We need to stick to that idea as long as we can because it will make us stronger physically, mentally, emotionally, spiritually, and even boost our confidence levels. Believing can be difficult to sustain, judging by whether or not our effort is proceeding smoothly, but it is also the factor that makes us who we are. A belief is a large commitment because we have to take an idea and stick to it no matter what.

20

BELIEVE

It is evident that strength comes with many positives and negatives all at once. We are all capable of reaching the next step toward what we desire, but the level of work it takes to get there can seem impossible. Be that as it may, no matter how difficult the task is, we can't just give up on it. If we do, some observers might assume that we are not trying and are even throwing away the progresses we have made already. That's kind of a cynical way of looking at it, but in some scenarios, that is the way people think. As hard as it is to stay strong during such a mental battle with oneself, we have to see it through to the end.

Some of us look at difficult situations with confidence, but others may see them as inspiring fear. Fear stands in the way of reaching that final point. Sometimes, it is so strong that it can keep us from approaching the task in another way. Confronting the feared issue is better than holding a question in the back of your mind and thereby leaving out any room for the possibility that the situation will get better, and it will not let your confidence blossom or even go through with something that really is possible. This can slow someone down until hopefully they realize it and then finally go forth with another kind of task. I've had some people talk to me about things they struggle with emotionally or even through a subject they struggle with in school. Here is where I try to talk with them and discuss other ways they can approach their situation or even just try to make them feel better.

People sometimes do seek me out for advice because what I say makes them gain confidence. Sometimes I wonder what things would be like if I didn't have the level of faith that I do. I often reminisce about the possibilities that may not have come to me if I did not have the attitude that I do. I wouldn't have so many friends and family who support me, would never have made the strides and improvements that I achieve every day, and I wouldn't inspire as many people as I have. Also, I wouldn't have recovered the way I did if my family wasn't so close to me. That's the most rewarding part of where I am at this point. Had I not had so much support and so many people there for me, I wouldn't be the person I am today. The same is true of my doctors at both hospitals; if they had not been so committed as to recognize how critical my condition was, I wouldn't have survived, let alone be where I am today. That's what the doctors at Boston Medical Center said; I always had somebody with me. I have come to accept my limitations right now, but that does not mean at all that I am anywhere near ready to stop trying to get better. I am fully aware that some things can only be of existence if enough effort is put into it, and why stop there?

There is a light that shines for anyone. For most, it is like seeing the embers after a fire; it's small but hasn't quite gone out yet. At other times, it can be a flickering flame that we all need to keep alive. That burning desire wants to hang in there and last as long as it can. There is only one way to see what's waiting underneath, and people have to believe they can reach it.

Improvement always takes more effort, and along with that, there must be a level of determination, as well as probable frustration, that will make you work harder. It can be annoying, but the truth is the drive is all part of the journey. Think about it as a test: you can be flying through it, but all of a sudden, you get stuck on a problem. Do you keep working or just give up on it? You keep working or come back to it later. As you work through the problem, the light of success gets brighter and brighter.

Sometimes, taking time feels as if it slows you down, but the delay is worth it because you can make sure you're getting it right. In life, it is usually best to take things slowly and make sure that you are doing the ethical or logical thing so that the outcome is the most accurate. At times, we may reach our breaking point, and that's okay too. In some instances, the best way to get there isn't running to it all at once. Falling apart emotionally on occasion is healthy because while it may make us feel as if we're not working to overcome our pain, it allows us to take a break from all our effort so that the struggle doesn't become an obstacle in our heads and let ourselves release the tension that is contracting our minds and bodies. No one wants to suffer a meltdown, but sometimes, unfortunately, it is what we need. That is true not just for people who have gone through a life-threatening injury, but for anyone in the world, whether the issue is about school, a bad relationship, a death, or even a fight with a friend. All this is part of what makes the circle of life go on.

Not only does believing in yourself guide you through the darkest hours, but it also can enable you to see possible things that were unimaginable before. This is the kind of thing that makes people the happiest as they can be surprised to think they can't do it one minute and then the next actually successfully execute it. Belief can come in different forms: the belief that there are bigger and better things out there in the world to take advantage of, the belief that fuels self-confidence, and even the kind that pushes you to try something one way, and even if you fail, it enables you to imagine other ways in which to go about succeeding in it. That is what's so beneficial about belief in yourself even if it takes much longer than you expected.

Whether or not there is any probability of knowing what makes sense to believe, we all have our own way of looking at different possibilities and chances that a solution could really come about and change life for the better. If something is hard or doesn't make sense to us at first, we all have to keep working at it because the only options are that it will work for us or it will not. No one wants a negative outcome, but it's better to figure it out than to spend our lives not knowing.

Unfortunately, this is far from any simple matter, but that's what makes the journey for understanding so much more rewarding. We shouldn't look at "the journey" as a burdensome trek toward the top that will take forever but rather see it as a way to track all the hard work and effort that has been put in. Everything in life takes some amount of effort, but the real defining question is how much we want, what is at the end of the rainbow, and how much we are willing to sacrifice our own time to obtain it. None of this is simple, but eventually, we can break the long climb into some small steps so that any of us can reach the top.

This whole process sounds like a long shot, but it can lead any of us toward the place we really want to be. Everybody deserves a chance to achieve something even if it seems unattainable. If we got used to people putting us down and let it get to us, well then it is least likely that they will succeed in doing that. However, if we stay strong and really devote all our ability to reaching that point, then the flickering light we see doesn't seem that far away. Even if we feel left behind because the journey is taking longer than antici-pated, we should remember that the whole thing is really beneficial because it shows us and others what we are capable of. Without all this experience, the point we really want to get to will be out of reach. Sometimes, it seems very far away; sometimes, it's waiting next door; and sometimes, it can be right in front of us.

People may see belief as something simple because it is just someone's point of view. However, it has so much more meaning than people think. As has been stated before, no one can presume the means by which an answer can be found. People have to realize that when they genuinely believe in something enough, there is more of a chance they can accomplish it. Everyone needs to believe in something that they have a commitment toward because that com-mitment will only grow as they think of alternative ways to approach things. Not every goal is required to have a complete solution in one way. There are other ways that we don't think about instantly. People may even see the belief itself as having one, but at any given moment, that focus can change into several different strategies and approaches. Although people might see belief in various ways that seem different at first, if anybody tests them out, they can see that they all come together in the end.

When something doesn't work out the first time, people know that usually they can try it again. Second chances are great because people know they can attempt the process in a different way. Here we know that when it doesn't work out, that doesn't make it the final answer. However, there are instances where there is only one shot for that person to finish what was started. I went through this and really shouldn't have survived because of everything that happened both with my accident itself and in those first weeks at Boston Medical Center. Looking at it now, and ever since I was conscious enough to understand, I realized I got a second chance at life. Initial recovery was a lot of hard work, and frustration at the same time; however, once I made enough small improvements, in almost no time I improved overall in so many different ways. I went from eating pureed to actual food. I went from walking on parallel bars to using a quad cane. And, of course, I went from struggling through fifth grade to managing better in middle and high schools and then to becoming a regular, more independent student rather than one who needed so much extra help in college. So many challenges tried to stop me again and again, but keeping this thought process alive made it possible for me to overcome all of them. None of that would have been possible without my second chance.

No matter what happens in the world or to us personally, people have to hold onto and believe in any possibilities. Accepting the reality of our misfortunes can be hard—it has been hard for me to accept the fact that I cannot do everything I used to do, but no matter how far away or unlikely whatever our objective is might seem, we need to keep it alive in our minds because it might actually work out. Kind of like when I was still comatose, my family stayed by my side even when I was in such bad shape because that small flame of hope that I'd wake up still was a single speck of light and possibility.

Anger can appear in any of us when we are frustrated about not having something the way we want it. I used to think that anger was a sign of weakness and an example of a bad attitude. Over time, I have learned that as much as anger is a negative, it's also something that keeps us moving and what motivates us to work harder. It's okay when we show anger about a situation as long as it passes. For me, when I've gotten angry in the past, I have tried to give myself a minute to be upset and then tried to move on, even if it meant I needed to seek a different way or even work longer than I had intended.

Recognizing where one stands takes a lot of faith alone, but actually going through with every little step also plays an important part in sustaining belief. It takes an enormous amount of effort to stick with an original plan. We can get so caught up in it that we may convince ourselves that it will work out in one specific way. We can only take so much adversity at once, but if we really believe we are on the right path, we take each little moment, test it out, and then, basing it on how we perceived it first, we can work out an additional way that can solve the problem at hand.

Even when we don't realize it, we are getting stronger and can create larger bits of progress every second of effort we put into it. Things happen, and sometimes we're not happy about them; we need to regard them as simply part of an obstacle we must get around. It's an opportunity to put ourselves to the test and see how much we can take before stopping. For me, it has taken longer than anyone thought to get my mobility back, and, of course, some people persist in a negative perspective that makes me feel that maybe I never will. However, using that as an opportunity to quit will just drag me down, and then I really will never know and always wonder. Instead, by taking things little by little, I know I am getting stronger every day, and my own strength is what will help muscles in my body grow and remember the way they acted before. It can be hard to stay strong because of the repetitive obstacles in our everyday lives as well. That is where commitment comes into play. If you are feeling that what you want is really important, you need to be ready for the journey that lies ahead.

Everyone knows about the ups and downs in life. It is only a matter of how we deal with the hiccups that can stop us in our tracks. Ups help to build our endurance; they let us know the road to continue following because our progress is going so well already. Downs can be seen as both a positive and a negative. A positive example would be that they help us move on to do something differently although as a negative influence they encourage us to stop putting in the effort. The truth is that if we were to stop in our tracks whenever something goes wrong, our road through life would keep taking detours, preventing us from moving toward the end of our voyages. As frustrating as the detours may seem, and how long it may take to get through them, the journey it requires could be beneficial. It can help us realize our ability to do things we wouldn't know we could do if there hadn't been an opportunity for them. If we ever seem stuck, it's important to try and claw our way out ourselves before depending on someone else. That's what can lead us to strengthen our abilities and motivation.

We can sometimes take life for granted without realizing it. If we commit ourselves to what we are doing, we not only recognize the hard work we've put into it, but also that we really can do the thing that seemed so hard to manage at first. Our path really is paved; it may just be under a layer of dust, so it's hard to find. Where it can go wrong is if we become so angry about something we can't conquer right away that we just don't finish it. This can happen all throughout life, but as long as there is room to stay strong and realize that the situation really can come around, eventually there will be room for the situation to change. Anything is possible; it's just a matter of dedicated time and effort.

I think about my life now. I think about all that's happened to me, and I think to myself that another person in my position might not be so motivated, and I myself sometimes wonder why I haven't given up. There have been many times when I ask myself that, and the conclusion is always that I don't know how high I can go before hitting my glass ceiling, but I want to try to get as high as possible. I don't want to go through life not knowing what could heal or change. I want people to see me as a role model. I want to be an inspiration, and I want to help anybody else who is going through a hard time.

Life itself is a mystery and a voyage all at once. People go through life searching for something of importance to them, trying it out, and if it doesn't work, they then move on to the next thing. They move on so as to avoid becoming frustrated if they repeatedly fail at the same thing. Whenever someone needs help on that voyage, it's important that they feel comfortable enough to ask others in order to be assured of the most beneficial guidance. As for myself, after I came home from the hospital, I wanted to do everything by myself and was a little resistant toward help. If I had stayed that mode all the time, then I definitely wouldn't stand where I do now.

Everything happens for a reason. That's true most of the time in my opinion; my viewpoint is supported in a book by Mira Kirshenbaum with that title that addresses the question of why things happen; I found her ideas very helpful. I'll never fully know the reason for what happened to me, but I'm happy to think that there is one and that it wasn't just a random thing that happened as it seemed at the time. Knowing this, I have become more willing to try harder things, take risks, continue working myself physically, be around my family, live life, keep pushing myself, and trying my best to help others. Every little event is crucial to how we live life. We have to find something that makes living worthwhile, whether it is knowing another path to take when our original plan doesn't work out or even reacting differently to a sudden change we're not happy about. Even with strength and dedication, sometimes the situation doesn't work to our advantage or the way we hope it will, but we have to stay open to the idea that eventually it will work out because, again, we'll never know until we try.

We all have certain expectations of our lives; if we find that circumstances change those expectations, we will never know if we can really live in our own new way and do things differently from what we planned until we have to. Sometimes, things get turned inside out or upside down, but there is usually a way they can get figured out. Unfortunately, we can't stop things from happening no matter how hard we try, but we need to recognize the impressive challenges people can surmount before being brought to their breaking point and, further, let others know how resilient it is possible to be. Until we understand what we need to do, it's okay to be upset (I'm the last person who'd say it's not okay to get frustrated). Actually, the most beneficial part of our lives can be right in front of us. We just might not see it at first.

Even with bobbles that throw us off, we still have to strive to reach an answer no matter how unlikely that seems to be for us. It's hard to hear for so long that improvements just take time, especially when we feel as if we are trying our hardest, but in these situations, the possible outcome is worth the perseverance, or at least it gives us the same feeling of confidence and satisfaction that helps push us to ways we had thought were out of reach. These challenges represent a test for each of us to see what we all really have the potential to do.

I've always thought it was interesting to consider how our life cycle really works and what we think of it. Life can be viewed in different ways. Some people see it as a journey, whereas others acknowledge it in a different light. Life is a gift that will almost always result in a big surprise. While it is a journey, it's also so much more. Life can be like a poker game where sometimes you have to use judgment to hold your cards close or play them with more caution, or it can be more like a game of Monopoly in which things happen by chance and the outcome of the game depends on the roll of the dice. There aren't dice in real life, but we similarly take chances every day.

As I said before, life is a journey, and with that come ups and downs. People wonder why some things happen when really all they need to do is take every little outcome as another form of a challenge that they need to endure. Hard things come and go, whether we like it or not. Therefore, we need to be prepared to use different thought processes and actions than what we had originally planned. Being prepared for the unplanned is one way in which we take on the concept of the fearful unknown. It is essential to stay strong-minded in confronting these concepts even though they are not always fun to think about or face, but that's what it takes in order to have the proper closing answer we are seeking.

With goal achieving comes a lot of responsibility, however. This idea can be tough to accept because people don't always want to take ownership if what they are attempting doesn't work out the way they want it to. Adhering to the theory "We'll never know unless we try" does imply accepting responsibility for what you have tried.

Everyone can do something amazing in life, but few can do it alone. Without all the support I got, in conjunction with how much I fought back against my limitation, I would not have made the progress I have. Recognizing my ability to overcome my obstacles with the assistance of others was an important indicator of my recovery process. I had to fight, but I couldn't do it alone. Without the proper exercises and my growing understanding of the many ways to focus on what my body could safely take, nobody would ever really know how far to push me. Still overtime, the way people pushed me lead me to do amazing things.

Most of us have aspirations as to what we can achieve even though they might seem too far off in the distance. It's an idea we look toward, and if we believe enough, we can even see beyond it as we strain to see the glimmer of possibility. Possibilities are stronger with the right people behind you.

Every life has separate paths with many choices. The only question is which way to go. These options can result in different ways to see a chance and seek the best way to execute it. Even if it seems far-fetched, when we choose a direction, even if we doubt it will work out, much to our surprise sometimes it does. It might even be the easiest process that we doubted would work in the first place. Occasionally, we can be blindsided by a situation and in such a way that we might give up on the path we are trying to follow. Taking an alternate path doesn't always seem like the best thing to do, especially if one is content with the current situation. Nevertheless, people do spend their lives trying their option and making different choices when they see that their path isn't exactly paved the way they originally thought it would be. We all want to know where our place is, but while we need to stay committed to what we are doing, we also need to be open to other things. I remember needing to start thinking this way when I realized I couldn't do things the same way that I used to.

Even when something seems far off and unlikely, we always need to hold on to that flicker of light even if we have to keep it in the back of our brain. We may think that our assessment of our current situation is set in stone when it really isn't; it may actually serve as a reminder to push us to work hard so that the dim light can morph into a burning flame. Hope is endless, and really sometimes, it is the last resort to turn to. We can't go on believing just what everybody says; often the answer lies in what we are willing to work for even if we have to sacrifice something. If you feel the need to question an assumption about your life, even if improvement seems impossible at first, you'll never know the potential outcome until you put the effort in and try.

One of the best things in life is recognizing that feeling of accomplishment. All of us face a challenging situation at some point in our lives. Even though it may seem to be nearly impossible to deal with at the time, it is important to commit ourselves to reaching an ending point wherever we can. Especially depending on the time and space we are in, frustration can get the better of us. Even if the amount of trouble we have with a task seems overwhelming, working hard to accomplish it can be the best feeling we can have. Frustration is a heavy burden, sometimes more than others, but when the job is completed, that wave of satisfaction in accomplishment seems to crash over us, pushing us along, rather than hitting us and pulling us under.

Frustration and difficulty can actually be in some ways positive things. Even though these feelings are usually viewed in negative terms, if we think about it, it is almost impossible to reach a desired outcome without these two emotions because they are the first indicators that something needs to change, and change will only happen if we really assert ourselves and work past each flaw we need to address. As long as we don't let frustration invade our heads too much, sufficient motivation can carry us through whatever is blocking our path. A task accomplished in a successful way gives us a broad rush of satisfaction and feeling of rejoicing.

When we encounter a distant obstacle, a barrier that is too far off, things may seem as if they won't work out. Leading the way forward isn't natural for everyone when they're in a position like this. In that situation, we have to keep exerting ourselves and trying to succeed every possible way. This becomes even more frustrating when we feel as if we've done everything possible. As hard as it sounds, however, most things can be done in an alternative way. It might take longer than we think, but that's when we need to be patient; maybe there is another way that has not even been seriously considered before. Obstacles are really hard to accept, but as long as we commit to the journey and try hard enough, there is nearly always a way to reach closer to the mountain's top, regardless of the climb.

We all recognizes the exciting feeling of succeeding. When we succeed at something we're good at, it's an extra top off to our self-confidence, but succeeding at something difficult for us is even that much more rewarding. If we face a path that is difficult for you and, further, are given discouraging feedback, we may struggle with it forever. However, if we transcend that negativity, fulfilling our ambition is even more exciting because we defeated the odds and took the chance, knowing the chance might be slim.

All too often, there are moments that many of us takes for granted without realizing it. Sometimes, we don't savor every moment or appreciate it for what it is. There have even been times when I have looked back on a task I completed but still felt unsatisfied because I didn't complete the job exactly the way that I had wanted to. Without having those moments of appreciating and really remembering our accomplishments, it's hard to move on because it might seem to us that we didn't work hard enough at it. Every little accomplishment in life should be recognized because it shows the work we have done to obtain it, and it shows proof of the determination it took in order to reach a conclusion.

In one sense, I'm happy with the person I am now because I can do so much more for others. Who I am now is much different from who I was back then before my world changed. I have grown into a more risk-taking, adventurous, courageous, and action-seeking person. Though I'm happy, I'm not about to stop working to become even better. It's hard to believe that one event can change your whole world and self-outlook, but my life-altering experience really made me appreciate more things and want to reach out more to others, not necessarily to those in a similar position physically but to anyone who needs any sort of help or guidance. There's so much left that is great about life that one event turning your world upside down actually doesn't seem that bad compared to everything else. I hope my words inspire you as much as life has inspired me.

Now you know my approaches in life and my story. I know that it's not the happiest one, but I thought it was important, for both me and others, to write about it. When people ask me what my story is, now I can simply hold out this book and say, "Here it is." My hope is that whenever readers finish this story, it will encourages them to go out and make the most of their lives.

What's next for me? Well, maybe that will be a new book.

Finally, I want to leave you with the same messages I hoped to get across through these pages. Life is a bumpy road, but everything makes us the people we are. We will all endure many hardships, but it is important to see them all the way through before turning the other cheek. I have completely evolved from the person that I was that horrible day in 2003. Fate has caused me many twists and turns instead of keeping me going in a straight direction, but it has evened out in time. Life can be very complicated, but we can get through it with distinction. It just takes commitment, perseverance, and strength.

The last skating competition the week before my accident

Family trip to New York City—Neill, and Lara in New York City after I moved home from Spaulding

John Passarini and I at the Katie Lynch Purple Shoes Challenge in 2004

My Associates degree college graduation cap

Grant Russum and I at the first Love Your Brain Retreat

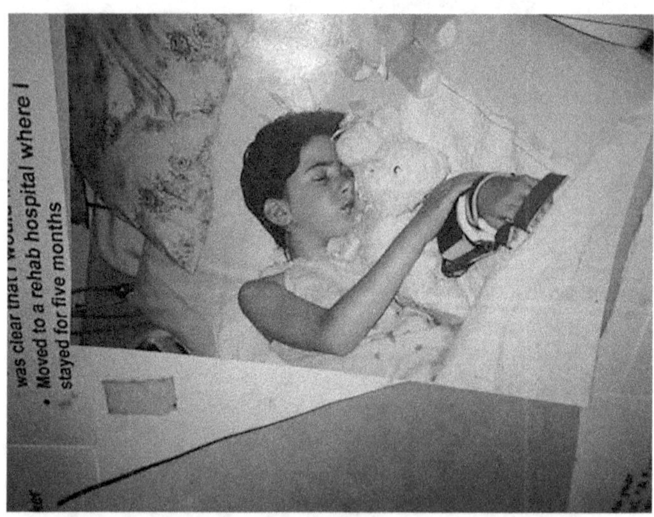

My first days at Spalding Rehabilitation Hospital while still comatose

Adam Pearce, Kevin Pearce, and me

My second time hand cycling alongside Bob
Shelton in the Burlington Marathon 2016

Holding my medal from the half marathon in 2017

Ross Lilley, Josh Lilley, and me at the Auction
for AccesSportAmerica 2016

Kathleen Barry and I at the cottage we rent in Goose Rocks 2016

Kathleen brought me back to visit Bobby's Ranch in 2017.
I hadn't been there since my accident 14 years before. I
needed to prove to myself that I wasn't afraid anymore.

Feeling the breeze windsurfing at the Spaulding with
AccesSportAmerica at the dock outside Mass Eye and Ear in 2016

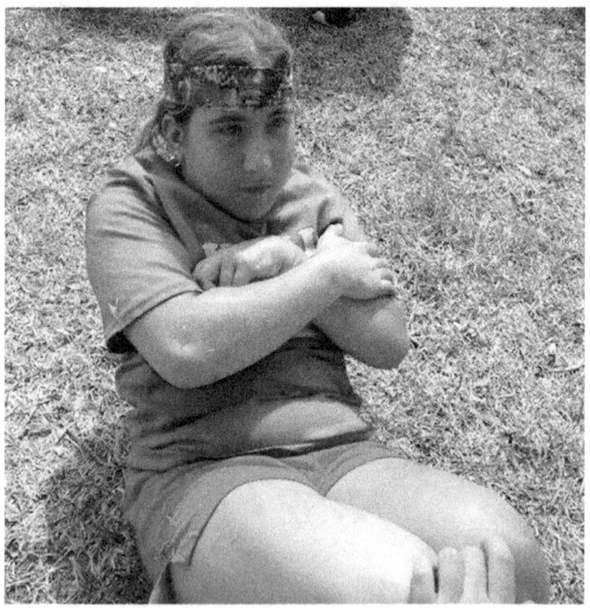

Sit-ups at Sports Camp in 2014

Admiring the Parthenon in Greece Summer 2014

Walking up to the Parthenon at the Acropolis in
Greece with Dad in Summer of 2014

Horseback riding with Zeno Mountain Farm in 2015

Family photo at Mom's Ballet Recital 2016 Neill Shelton, Bob Shelton, Mara Shelton, Lara Shelton, and me

Shirt given to me by Sage's mom after the first Love Your Brain retreat

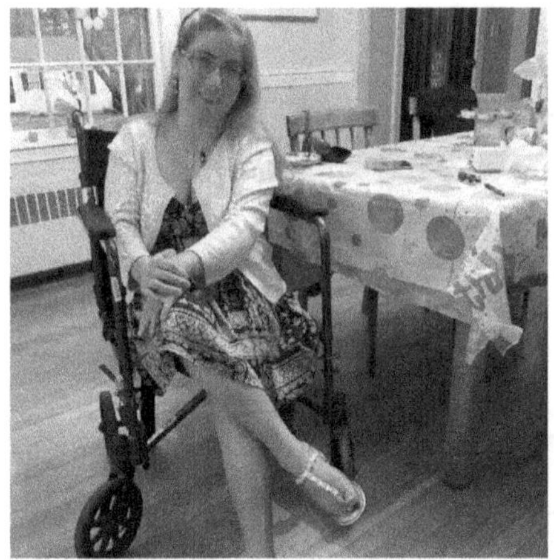

Marina lives today in Massachusetts. She is an advocate for people with disabilities and continues to do amazing things. She also enjoys being with her family and cheering her brother and sister on during their skating shows. She loves doing adaptive sports. She still under-stands her limitations, but that is not stopping her from trying.

9 798891 578753